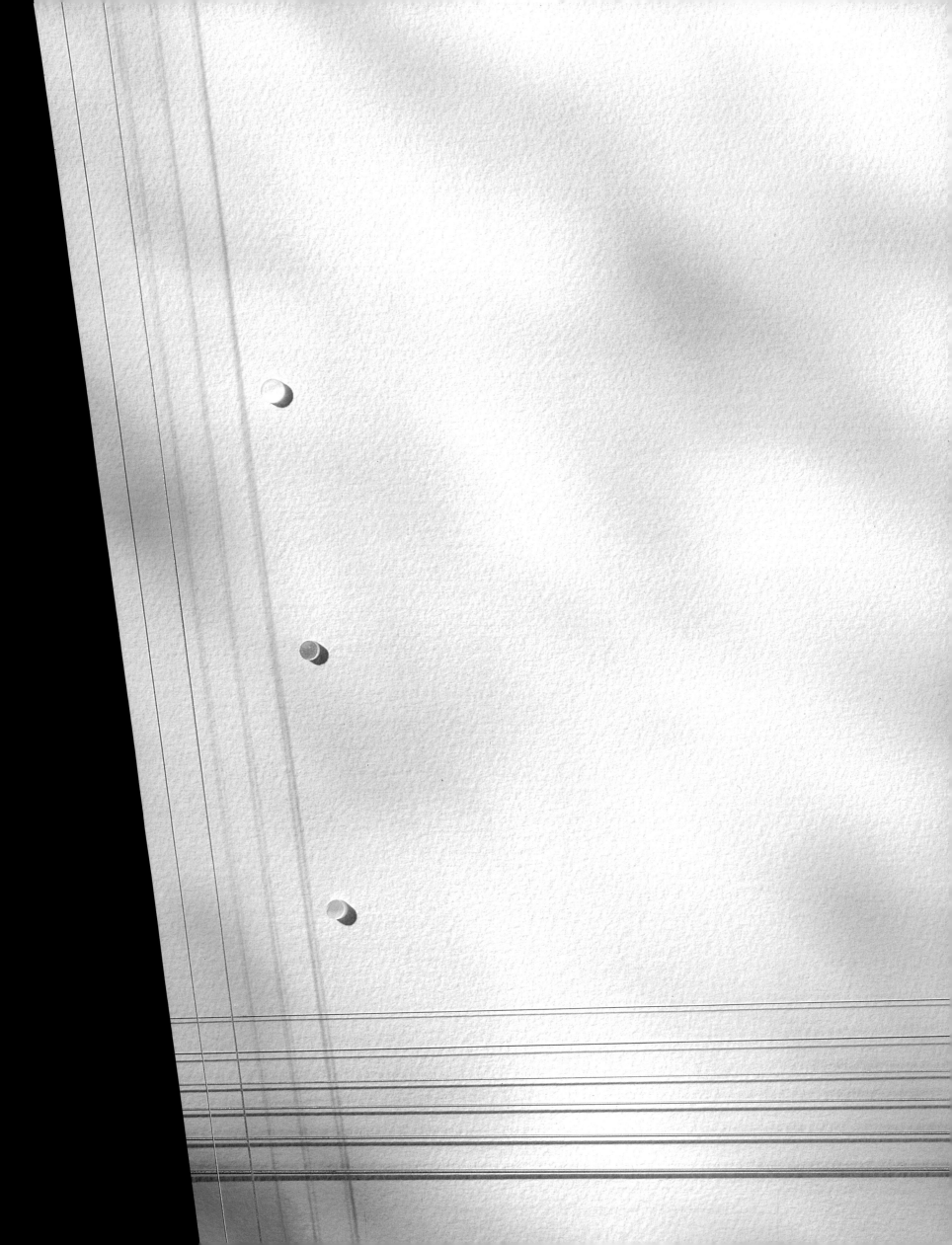

FERRINGTON Guitars

Featuring the Custom-made Guitars of
Master Luthier **Danny Ferrington**

Design and Photography
Nancy Skolos and Thomas Wedell
Introduction
Linda Ronstadt
Profile
Orville Schell
Editor
Kate Giel
Editorial Director
Nicholas Callaway
Compact Disc Mastering
George Massenberg

HarperCollins*Publishers* and Callaway Editions 1992 A BoundSound™ Book

•

I grew up in a family where the acoustic guitar was looked upon as a very personal instrument. Everybody in our house played the guitar at least a little, and depending upon the time of day or the mood, you could usually find a guitar either in our living room, surrounded by a crowd of people taking turns playing and singing, or behind a closed door in one of the bedrooms, where somebody would be sitting alone on the bed playing quietly

I think music is almost a biological necessity for people. It's a tool that we have developed to help us make sense out of all the things we see taking place around us each day. Music is not simply decoration for our ears; it's something that stands apart from all our other experiences because it provides one of our most intuitive pathways toward sanity and health. And listening to the soothing sound of a guitar is one of the best ways for people to find their way back to something good.

Danny Ferrington must know all this because he has a way of taking a musician's dreams and translating them into a guitar that really represents the personality of its user. The dedication and devotion that he lavishes on his guitars has been plain whenever I've seen him working in his shop. To watch Danny build a guitar is like witnessing the evolution of something living as it moves quickly through the early stages of development toward the more meticulous and time-consuming processes of refinement and perfection that come later. It's a strange combination of slapdash slamming together of things and incredibly fine, precise work, but when he is finished, the result is poetry.

Whenever I've ordered a guitar from Danny, I've had the feeling that I was launching something that would have a lifespan that would probably exceed my own. A Ferrington guitar may reflect the personality of its purchaser, but in the long run, I feel that we are merely custodians for the instruments that he makes. In truth, each of his guitars is a unique creation that has the potential to bring an almost limitless amount of music into the world.

Linda Ronstadt
April 1992

Profile

by Orville Schell

•

Danny in his current shop, 1991

"It's a complete pleasure for me just being able to come down here to my shop, listen to music, and cut and glue wood," Danny Ferrington told me while sitting in his workshop, his sing-song Louisiana twang reminding me that he may be *in* Los Angeles but is still not completely *of* it. "I mean, I just love being down here alone making my guitars," he added, drawling out the word "love."

At first glance it was hard to see why Ferrington would be so enamored of this particular workspace, an unimposing structure that looks as if it had once been a garage and is located in a back-alley parking lot behind a Santa Monica, California restaurant. A passerby looking in through the open double doors would see a homemade workbench covered with carpet remnants and littered with scraps of wood and strangely shaped tools. But just to see what Ferrington was cutting and glueing together would not be to discern what makes him love to be there so much. Moreover, the shop has an almost junky, unkempt feeling to it. In the rear stand a dusty band saw, drill press, and air compressor. The furnishings consist of a few rickety old bar stools with torn cushions tied onto them, an old stereo surrounded by a large collection of records and CDs, and a porch swing hung in the entranceway looking out through the double doors past a dumpster into the parking lot. Except for the litter of guitar cases cluttering the floor, passersby might think they were looking in on someone's incipient garage sale rather than the workshop of one of the world's most renowned master luthiers, or guitar makers, who has made instruments for such legendary musicians as Ry Cooder, J. J. Cale, Eddie Van Halen, David Hidalgo, Johnny Cash, Lindsey Buckingham, Jackson Browne, Leo Kottke, Linda Ronstadt, Eric Clapton, Richard Thompson, Emmylou Harris, Ricky Lee Skaggs, Crystal Gayle, Waylon Jennings, Elvis Costello, Pete Townshend, J. D. Souther, and Hoyt Axton, to name a few.

Danny climbing into his first Santa Monica shop, 1985

Danny Ferrington has never been taken as much by the outer trappings of his craft as by the craft itself. And he has always been somewhat cavalier, even eccentric, in the choosing of his workplaces, as if where he is does not really matter in making a good stringed instrument. At his last shop, health buffs on their way for a workout at the Lifeplus Dance and Exercise Studio in a commercial section of Santa Monica were sometimes surprised to see a man shinnying up a rope dangling down the side of an automotive paint store, and then slipping through into a garret. The figure was neither a Spiderman trainee nor a thief on the prowl but Danny Ferrington, going to his shop on weekends or after hours, when he likes to work and when the Santa Monica Automotive Colors shop, over which he rented his space, was closed, blocking off the staircase. Much to the bemusement of passersby, Ferrington solved the dilemma of off-hours ingress and egress by simply hanging a rope out his loft door and pulling himself up and sliding down like a commando.

Now that he has moved, he no longer needs to engage in such airborne gymnastics. And since he is on ground level, if he wants solitude now, he pretty much has to work at night. Although Ferrington refuses to have a phone in his workshop because he doesn't want the disturbance, his southern gregariousness makes him vulnerable to the endless interruptions of people who pop in throughout the day just to say hello and chat as if they were all living in a small town, rather than in the sprawling metropolis of Los Angeles. Among them are the antique furniture maker next door who is fascinated by Ferrington's deft way with wood; the restaurant owner in the front of his shop who is happy to supply him with coffee, tea, and muffins in exchange for emergency repairs on doors that suddenly fall off their hinges and kitchen fans that unexpectedly go on the blink; the young architect at the end of the alley who appreciates his unusual sense of design; and the endless guitar buffs and musicians who troop in and out to see what Ferrington is up to. And he is always up to something new.

Danny Ferrington is as unorthodox about making guitars as he is about his workshops. Instead of being the stereotypical Old World craftsman one might imagine a master luthier to be—a bearded, slow motion Gepetto-like elder with wire-rimmed glasses and a leather apron—Ferrington is only thirty-nine years old and dresses in jeans, T-shirts, and a leather jacket. Rather than working with costly antique implements, he either makes most of his tools himself or just buys them at Sears, while most of the paints and sealers he uses come from an auto shop. What is more, he has no compunction about using power tools when necessary to craft his exquisite instruments. "There's no room for brown rice or granola on any of my guitars," he once told me.

Although he stands only five-foot-six, Ferrington is bullishly strong. He has rarely met his match in arm wrestling, and I have seen him climb a forty-foot pine tree without branches in a matter of seconds.

"I grew up in Louisiana, and my earliest years were spent in a small bayou town called Enterprise," Ferrington told me as we sat at his workbench and sipped tea one day. "Our place was nine miles off the paved road, had no running water and no telephone. The nearest neighbor was two miles away, and we had to ride a ferryboat to get to school. But we always had a tightly knit family. I had a brother, Dudley, and a sister, Jan, and at one point I had all my grandparents and great-grandparents alive at the same time."

Ferrington's father, Loyd, was a cabinet maker who at one time had played guitar and bass in a local country-and-western combo, and Danny's first experience working with wood came from helping his father in his shop at home after the family moved from Enterprise to Monroe, a somewhat larger Louisiana town

Danny (center front) with McGuffee grandparents and cousins, 1956

Amy and Loyd Ferrington, 1951

Dudley, Jan, and Danny (holding record album), Christmas 1957

"Oh, we knew he had a gift," remembered his mother, Amy, in her good-hearted honey-sweet Louisiana drawl during a visit to see her son in L.A. "When he was real little Danny'd take a set of Tinkertoys out and make things that were so amazing I wouldn't want to take them apart. He was always fiddling around with something. I remember one night I came home from work to find that he'd gotten some kind of catalogue for guitar parts. I was busy trying to fix dinner for the family, and he was telling me how he wanted to send away for stuff to make a guitar. Well, I wasn't going to say anything discouraging to him or nothing, because he was just ten or eleven. But I was thinking, 'Poor little thing! He thinks he's going to make a guitar!' Little did I know!" When either Loyd or Amy speaks about their son, the warmth and pride evident in their voices is unalloyed.

Loyd Ferrington (right) with high school bandmates, 1947

"When he was a kid he used to make little carts, birdhouses, and windmills," Loyd fondly remembers of his son. "From the time he was about thirteen or fourteen he got off that school bus each afternoon, had some milk and cookies, and then came straight into my shop to go to work until dark. He's always been able to take a piece of wood and do almost anything with it."

Danny's grandparents gave him his first guitar when he was about twelve. "From the moment I got that instrument, I was always wanting to tinker with it," remembered Ferrington. He got his chance to do even more tinkering when a man named Doc Savage, who repaired guitars in Monroe, allowed him to help in his shop. Danny hung around Doc Savage until at last he actually let him repair some of the guitars himself.

When Danny entered college, taking a general business course, he almost instantly knew that a future in business was not for him. "I hated it!" he recalled, squinching up his face and furrowing his brows. Indeed, it is almost impossible to imagine Danny Ferrington in a classroom studying accounting. "I really didn't know what I wanted to do, but I knew it wasn't going to be business," he emphatically recalled. "All I knew was that I could make cabinets and had a way with wood."

Danny at the Old Time
Pickin' Parlour, 1977

Danny with Grand Ole Opry fiddler
Charlie Collins (front left) and
Mike Pierson (back left), 1976

Danny and Linda Ronstadt, 1985

When Ferrington heard that the Old Time Pickin' Parlour in Nashville, Tennessee, a vintage acoustic guitar repair shop and an after-hours bluegrass club, was looking for another apprentice, he jumped at the chance.

"They were offering $2 an hour, but that didn't bother me," he recalled. "I'd been reading in my bluegrass magazines about all the famous stars like Vassar Clements, Roy Acuff, Charlie Collins, and Bill Monroe who used to go over and play there after the Grand Ole Opry, so I was really eager. And when I actually got up there, I felt as if I had gone to bluegrass heaven."

"We've always been real close, and it broke my heart when Danny left home," Loyd Ferrington wistfully told me when we talked recently in Los Angeles. "After he went I never could find anybody with whom I could work in the shop as well as him. Working with Danny was like being part of a musical combo, it's not easy just to replace one member. But because I knew he had a gift that needed to be developed, I always wanted to support him."

At age twenty-three, Ferrington started working in Nashville at the Old Time Pickin' Parlour with the famed acoustic guitar maker Randy Wood. "I learned almost everything I know from him," he recalled reverently as we sat in his present shop. "Randy was a man of few words, but he had a kind of magical touch when it came to wood, and he was generous with his knowledge. At night when they'd all be playing downstairs in the Pickin' Parlour, I'd go up to the shop and just watch Randy work. Then I'd try and imitate him. Most people look at a guitar and wonder how in the hell you get something like that out of a log. It's actually not all that hard, once you know how." He laughs.

Danny with Randy Wood, 1977

Danny's first guitar, built
for Paul Craft, 1977

Ferrington's first guitar was made for singer-songwriter Paul Craft, who has penned such hits as "Keep Me from Blowing Away" and "Midnight Flyer."

"I said to him, 'Hey, Paul, I'll tell you what. I'll make you an instrument, and if you don't like it, you don't have to pay for it.' Well, he just loved that guitar, and things started snowballing for me."

After being in Nashville for five years, Ferrington began to get restless. "By that time, I had made guitars for every picker with money–and some without," he recalled. "But in my work, I had come to a dead end, and I really needed to try something new."

"Randy Wood said he'd seen a lot of guys come and go through his shop, and that some had the right idea about how to make instruments but couldn't do it with their hands, while others could do the craftsmanship but didn't have any idea in their head what they wanted to do," Loyd told me of his son's tenure in Nashville. "He said Danny was the only one that really had what it takes both in his head and his hands."

In 1980 Danny left Nashville for Los Angeles, where he ultimately ended up sharing a house with Linda Ronstadt, whom he had first met through Paul Craft at a concert. Far from being overwhelmed by the big city, he thrived in Los Angeles. "A lot of people thought that a country boy like me would hate L.A. with all its glitz and smog," he said, smiling broadly. "But I loved it from the start!"

Ferrington's strong sense of family and his deep Louisiana roots stood him in good stead in L.A. Unlike many other outsiders who readily succumbed to Tinseltown's corruptions, Ferrington kept his balance and continued his craft, albeit in a new and more energized fashion. There were no drugs or alcohol, no Mercedes convertibles with car phones, no manicurists, no personal body trainers for Danny Ferrington. He was dazzled by all the film stars, musicians, and entertainment executives with whom he soon found himself rubbing shoulders, but at the same time he never lost his down-home values and, most important, never stopped making guitars. It was a paradox that this city, which in many ways offended him with its excesses, also provided him with inspiration. He loved its exciting energy, artistic effervescence, and the fact that it had become one of the epicenters of the pop-music earthquake that was shaking the world.

"L.A.'s a fountainhead of musicians, which makes it easy for me to get a drink whenever I need to," said Danny, describing his curious relationship to L.A. "It's a necessary evil, but I really like it here!" Then he added, with only partial facetiousness, "Besides, the climate here is just perfect for making guitars. Because the weather isn't changing all the time, the wood doesn't crack."

The artistic and social yeastiness of the L.A. music and entertainment scene and the solitude of his shop seem to complement each other perfectly.

"Sometimes I'm sitting at some party loaded with the hip of the hippest musicians and movie stars, and I think to myself, 'This is as far from Monroe, Louisiana as a boy can get!' I love it, but I'm always happy to get back to my work."

What began to turn Ferrington into more than just another traditional, albeit extremely talented, luthier was his urge to push conventional acoustic guitars out of the tradition-bound rut. As the center of the recording industry, and increasingly of the revolution in contemporary American design as well, L.A. was the perfect place for him to begin pondering new ways of looking at acoustical stringed instruments, which had stubbornly maintained their rigidly traditional shape for centuries.

"I knew that if I began fooling around with the shape of acoustic instruments in Nashville, they'd start making fun of me," said Danny with a smirk. "But in L.A., where anything goes, people would say, 'Hey! Show me something weird!' And that's what I wanted to hear."

It was during the early eighties, as Danny was finding his way in the Southern California music world, that he started experimenting with both the design and sound of instruments by making asymmetrically shaped guitars. One of the challenges he set for himself was to break down the gulf which had grown up between rock-and-rollers, who were wedded to their electric guitars, and folksingers and bluegrass musicians, who remained wedded to their traditional acoustic instruments. To make acoustic guitars appear a little more interesting, he started to borrow some of the avant-garde designs that had already overtaken the solid-body electric guitar industry.

Danny and Don Was (holding his bass), 1991

"I wanted to try and get all the electric rock-and-rollers interested in acoustics again," Danny explained with a smirk. "They had been treating them as if the instruments had leprosy, and I wanted to prove that just because you have an acoustic guitar doesn't mean that you have to play 'Puff the Magic Dragon' all night. So what I did was to make an acoustic which was styled after an old electric Gibson Explorer—really an outrageous shape for an acoustic." What surprised Danny about this experiment was that the guitar not only looked good, it also had a good sound. "I took it to some rock-and-rollers when I finished and said, 'Here, have a try.' And when they crouched right down like they were playing on their electrics, I knew I was onto something."

Soon, almost all of Danny's new custom acoustics—which usually take two weeks to a month to make and cost from $2,000 to $3,000—had become bold experiments in size, shape, design, tonal quality, inlay pattern, and finish. The end products are masterpieces of fine and delicate craftsmanship, so when I first watched Danny at work in his shop, I was surprised by the voraciousness with which he leans into the task of making rigid pieces of wood yield to his hand. For instance, as he begins to shape a piece of wood for the neck of a guitar, he fairly attacks it with a huge rasp

Danny shaping wood for the neck of a guitar 1991

that looks rough enough to belong to a farrier. Even when he works with the cardboard-thin pieces of wood that make up the tops, sides, and backs, he goes about his task at such high speed that you wonder how he avoids doing something wrong. Only through careful watching is his deftness revealed. He has a sureness of hand that is so certain about what tool he grabs, where he cuts, or what he sands that one is left wondering if Danny Ferrington couldn't build a pretty respectable instrument in a completely dark room.

"There is a unique tactile thing about each piece of wood," Ferrington explained. "You have to form an individual relationship with that piece of wood almost as if it were a person. By now the wood-working process of guitar making has gotten to be such a second nature to me that I don't even use any templates or jigs, and I hardly even measure things, or use calipers to shape fretboards. I just eyeball the wood, and do it. My guitar making has gotten so spontaneous that sometimes I don't quite know where the instruments come from. All I know is that when I make cuts they go where I want them to until the guitar is in front of me."

As we talked, Danny suddenly pulled out a new fretted bass guitar he recently made for Don Was, record producer and member of the band Was (Not Was), and started plucking on it.

"Don wanted an acoustic bass with frets, but he didn't want that clacking sound of the strings hitting metal," explained Danny, running his hand up the neck of the big guitar. "He asked me if I couldn't make the frets out of wood. At first I was worried because I knew that they would wear down with use. But then we both thought, what the heck? If they wear down, I'll just replace them with new ones." As Danny described the process, it all sounded so easy. But then, almost everything Danny says about making guitars sounds deceptively easy.

"I love the instrument because it sounds like an upright bass," Was later told me. "Danny gets right in there with the interaction . . ." Then, instead of finishing his sentence, he began thumping away on his new bass in satisfaction as if this was the most eloquent testimony to the instrument.

"Stradivari made maybe one thousand violins and cellos and a few violas and guitars. And do you know something? Every one was different," Danny told me back in his shop, making me smile at the thought that a Louisiana country boy has been inspired by the great seventeenth-century Italian violin maker. "Stradivari didn't use any formulas. Actually, no one quite knows what made Stradivari's stringed instruments so great. Almost every year you hear a new theory. But I think they all miss the boat. Stradivari just had a wonderful but unanalyzable ability with wood. That's probably why no one has been able to copy him."

Stringed instruments make sound when air is moved by the vibrations of a plucked or bowed string. Just as the mouth of a singer is a projector for sound made by vibrating vocal cords, so the wooden structure of an acoustic guitar is an amplifier of sound made by the vibrating strings stretched across its surface.

"When a string is plucked, the top of a guitar moves in and out like a diaphragm and agitates air, producing a much higher volume of sound than a string could alone," Ferrington explained as he twanged a bass string on one of his big baritone guitars, and then let it resonate throughout his shop. The agitated air excites the thin top of a guitar so that it too begins to vibrate. Because the top, or soundboard, is so very important in reflecting sound outward, most luthiers use spruce, a wood that is perfect because of its grain structure. Hard, dark vertical grain layers give strength and conduct sound all the better because they are laminated in suspension between alternating layers of porous, softer cellulose.

While most sound comes from the top of a guitar, a whole other range of tone passes from the neck to the inside of the instrument where it bounces off the sides and the back—made of hard or soft woods like maple, rosewood, and mahogany, which do not easily vibrate—and issues forth again from the circular hole in the guitar's center. Each of these woods has its own characteristic sound properties, and the task of the luthier is to match the right wood and construction technique to the quality of sound that a musician wants from his instrument. The thinner the top, the more resonant the instrument. However, since the taut strings exert enormous pressure on the frail top—as much as two hundred and fifty pounds of tension—guitar makers must reinforce all instruments with slender interior braces that act something like the ribs in wooden boats. And since bracing dampens sound, the art of a good luthier is in no small measure in knowing where to place these braces, and how strong to make them.

"The top must be in a perfectly balanced state of tension, braced enough so that it won't collapse under the tension of the strings, but weak enough to vibrate and create a good tone," explained Danny as we peered inside one of his instruments at the slender interior network of ribbing that keeps it together. "It's easy to make a guitar which will never fall apart by just loading it up with heavy bracing, but its tone won't be very interesting. A truly good guitar must be right on the edge of breaking apart."

Interior braces on the top and back of the guitar, 1991

Danny with first asymmetrical guitar, built for Nick Lowe, 1980

"There is no rule for bracing," Danny continued. "After I see how thick the sides are going to be and how big the top of the guitar is, there is just something that impels me to make the bracing a certain way and a certain thickness."

By experimenting with different shapes in his L.A. shop, Ferrington also made another important discovery. He knew that when plucked, a string not only vibrates to the pitch to which it has been tuned, but also sets off a series of overtones. These extra tones sound natural to the human ear, but when recorded create difficulties for sound engineers.

"The problem with a perfectly symmetrical acoustic guitar is that when you record it, you get a muddy sound which is usually too 'bassy,' "explained Danny, picking up one of his own guitars and striking the low E-string. "Studio engineers have to doctor the sound up electronically by equalizing it, or enhancing the treble and muting the bass. But what I inadvertently discovered is that by making both the guitar bodies and the holes on the front asymmetrical, I could cut out a lot of these extra tones and get a much flatter or purer response. As a result, most recording engineers just love my acoustic guitars."

For Ferrington, the discovery that asymmetrical shapes worked for acoustical instruments opened the door to an almost limitless number of new design possibilities. With this new discovery that he could push acoustic guitar making out into a new aesthetic as well as tonal frontier, he began to pay real attention to the broader spectrum of ways that he could customize his instruments to fit the individual personalities of his clients. Prior to Danny's arrival in L.A., the only guitars that had broken through the traditional "hips," "waists," and "cheeks" design were solid electrics. Unlike acoustic guitars, which depend on the hollow body of the instrument as an amplifier, solid-bodied electric guitars create sound by electronically amplifying the vibrations directly from the strings. When Ferrington found that he could make hollow acoustic guitars that were as unorthodox in design as electrics but which had good sound, the discovery set him free to experiment with all kinds of shapes: straight edges, square corners, elliptical curves, cutaways, and a host of other uncategorizable and intriguing configurations.

"I think the design of an instrument should be as pleasing as the sound," proclaimed Ferrington. "They should be like old Cadillacs—beautiful, but still capable of getting you there."

But having proved to himself that both shape and tone were variables that he could play around with, Danny found himself with much greater latitude in custom-making his instruments to fit both the musical needs and the aesthetic tastes of the musicians for whom he was making custom guitars.

"I'm not interested in making the same guitar over and over again," he told me. "I want to throw convention out and fit the guitar right to the person. I can't make anonymous guitars. For me, making a guitar has become a collaborative process with the musician who is going to play it. My clients are my muse. They inspire me to create instruments that I wouldn't make otherwise, and that they couldn't get anywhere else."

"He inspires me too," virtuoso guitarist Ry Cooder, who owns five Ferringtons, told me. "We live in a musical world where everything has gone generic. You think you've seen everything until Danny comes over. He's ingenuity, craft, and energy all in one. He breaks out of all the old stultifying patterns, and somehow gets you into something you really want even though you might not even have known it before he came over."

"People like that have ideas about what they want," acknowledged Danny. "And my job is to interpret those ideas and make them a reality for them."

Ferrington spends so much time listening to music, hanging out with musicians around L.A., and going to clubs and concerts that often, before an artist even orders an instrument, he already has a good intuitive feel for that person's musical style and personality.

"Nothing makes me happier than to work with someone in this collaborative process to get the design, the tone, the color, the inlays–the whole thing–just right for that particular musician," Danny told me with a sincerity that is unmistakable.

The one-hour guitar, built in 1988

"He's made some amazing guitars," acknowledged J. J. Cale, who knew him back in Nashville and has bought three acoustics from him. "He knows his woodwork, but he's a designer too. He's always trying to come up with something different. Sometimes his stuff is pretty crazy, but the thing is that you can actually play it! Now, everyone's trying to imitate him."

"I have to like a musician and their music before I can really make a good guitar for them," Danny insisted. "For me it's a very personal thing. But what I like about it is that often musicians learn a little more about what they want by working with me to design them a guitar. Most musicians are on a constant and seemingly endless quest to find an instrument which best suits them. For instance, Eric Clapton, who bought two guitars from me, already had about sixty other instruments."

"When Danny makes a guitar, it ends up being personalized for the musician not only in the way it sounds but in the way it looks," Linda Ronstadt, who owns two Ferringtons, told me. "Somehow he is able to dream your guitar into shape, color, and sound, so that it not only responds to you but is in a sense an extension of your personality. He makes instruments which actually look like the people who own them. When he did one for Waylon Jennings, for instance, it was huge, black, and angular. I mean, it was Waylon Jennings!" She gave a little burst of laughter at the thought.

"It's something like writing a song together," Danny told me in trying to describe this ineffable process. "We go through every little element together, and when we're done, that musician will have a unique instrument which is technically, visually, and tonally tailored to that person."

Waylon Jennings's guitar, built in 1979

Reeves Gabrels with his baritone, 1992

"My wife got me a baritone Ferrington for our fifth wedding anniversary," David Bowie's Tin Machine band guitarist, Reeves Gabrels, told me, a tone of obvious warmth in his voice for Ferrington and the experience of having a custom guitar made by him. "It was such a thrill to go out to his shop, sit on the porch swing, choose the woods, talk about the design and inlays. I love that kind of melted look his guitars have. Most other guitar makers have one or two certain trademark things they do, and that's what you get, like it or not. But not Danny. He'll build you whatever you want. The challenge is really yours." He laughs. "You can quickly come right up against the limits of your own musical imagination."

As an experiment Danny once made what he calls a "one-hour guitar" for musical genius Ry Cooder. It consisted of a piece of three-quarter-inch plywood band-sawed into the silhouette shape of a guitar, with a factory neck bolted on and an old Fender bass pick-up taped at a slant under the strings with masking tape.

"It was a guitar that no one in his right mind would have made," Danny exclaimed.

"It's a killer!" exclaimed Cooder when I asked him about it. "Less is more with an electric guitar! And if there's less of it there's got to be more of you. You know, so much good guitar music was done by people who didn't have good instruments. That's a special sound that's hard to get these days."

For the English rocker Elvis Costello, Danny made a midnight-black guitar that looks as if its design has been borrowed from Georges Braque or Pablo Picasso. He made another, for singer Carlene Carter, that looks as if it has been squashed by something very heavy. And for Waylon Jennings he built a guitar with a cutaway at the bottom that makes it look as if someone has taken a bite out of it.

Eric Clapton's guitar, built in 1979

When I asked which of these collaborative experiences he remembers most fondly, Danny immediately said, "All of 'em." Then, after a pause he added, "Well, the guitars I made for Elvis Costello were pretty close to the top. I've hung out with him so much that we almost have a shorthand between us.

Texas-shaped headstock on J. D. Souther's guitar, built in 1982

Hoyt Axton's "sixteen angels" guitar, built in 1984

I know his musical roots, that he loves honky-tonk and that he's bluesy. So we sat down and designed him an instrument right here in L.A., and we really went out on a limb. It was black like an Everly Brothers guitar, with a mandolin scroll, tortoise shell pick-guard, and his name inlaid country western-style down the fretboard. When I sent it to Elvis and he propped it up at the end of the hall and looked at it all day, I just said to myself, 'This is it!' I don't know how to thank him for letting me make it."

Elvis Costello's second guitar, built in 1981

Kurt Cobain with his electric, 1992

Linda Ronstadt's guitar, built in 1980

Ferrington is also a master at inlaying and finishing his custom guitars in unique ways that leave his customers ecstatic. For actor and country singer Hoyt Axton he made a traditional-style acoustic inlaid on the neck and top with sixteen angels, all painstakingly cut out of mother-of-pearl with a jeweler's saw and routed into the woodwork. When he made Kathy Valentine of the Go-Go's a guitar, he inlaid it with the same heart and crossbones that she has tattooed on her arm. For J. D. Souther, who is from Amarillo, Texas, he crafted a black guitar with pink binding (trim) and a headstock shaped like the Lone Star State, with a mother-of-pearl star on the Panhandle to mark his hometown. Ferrington made singer Johnny Cash a guitar with gold inlays on the top. ("This guitar has renewed my interest in guitar playing," announced Cash.) And he inlaid a guitar with pink ribbons, bows, and cherubs for Linda Ronstadt.

Just as a birth is the beginning of the process of child-rearing, so for Ferrington, completing one of his new custom instruments is a starting point in rather than the end of a long-term relationship. Like a lifetime health insurance policy, Ferrington's relationship with his progeny guarantees its owner a lifetime of care. Over the years his instruments keep coming back to him for repairs, refurbishing, or just to be adapted to the changing preferences of their owners.

In 1980 Danny made a miniature guitar whose body was no bigger than a football for Pete Townshend to take with him on the road. When the top needed repairs this year, Townshend sent it back to Ferrington. Far from being irritated by such details, Ferrington seemed gladdened by the guitar's reappearance, much as a parent would welcome kids home from college at vacation time. When Michael Landau, a top session player who has recorded with everyone from Miles Davis and Rod Stewart to Linda Ronstadt and James Taylor, recently decided that he no longer wanted the skull and crossbones on his custom-made baritone guitar, Danny simply offered to run over to his house, pick up the instrument, and refinish it for him, gratis.

As Landau told me when I caught him at a studio recording session for Felix Cavaliere, of the sixties band The Rascals, "What's great about Danny is he's so hands-on. He's not like these other snobby guitar makers who say, 'Oh, you want one of my instruments? Well, first tell me who you've played for.' When Danny brought me my baritone, I took it right home, and wrote a song . . . about my Mom." He laughs.

As I was interviewing Ferrington, he was in the process of discussing a new guitar for Kurt Cobain, the lead singer of the popular new group Nirvana. Knowing that sometimes Cobain gets so into his music that he damages his instruments, I asked Danny how he felt about making a guitar for someone like that.

"I don't want people taking ice picks to my guitars, but stuff is going to happen in the line of duty," he responded matter of factly. "Cobain just gets unbelievably into his thing, but no problem! I'll just make him a guitar with a few extra screw-on necks. The real truth is that I don't care if they break my guitars up as long as they are using them. The most awful thought to me is that someone will buy one of my instruments and then never use it."

He began telling me about Johnny Cash, who has this big gold eagle on his belt buckle that chewed up the back of the guitar Ferrington made for him. "It looked like someone had clawed it with a gardening tool," Danny said. "Now, some people thought that was a sacrilege, but I love it and fixed his guitar right up because it showed me that Johnny was using it. If the musicians break 'em up a little, just as long as they use them, I'll fix them up. I'll even make 'em another," crows Danny cheerfully as if constructing a new instrument was no more formidable a task than baking a cake.

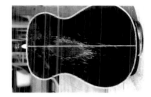

Chewed-up back of Johnny Cash's guitar, 1980

Danny and Johnny Cash, 1978

"For me a guitar is only viable if someone is creating music on it," he insisted almost dogmatically. "A guitar is a living thing, and without someone playing it, it's no better than a chair. I can't be really proud of one of my instruments until I hear it in a concert or on a record; until I know it's really bonded with someone. It would horrify me if collectors began buying my guitars to hang like paintings on the walls of their houses or in museums." He clutched the sides of his face in mock horror. "Ooooh, no! I wouldn't like that at all."

Johnny Cash's guitar, built in 1979

When I reminded him that he himself takes pride in the idea that the instruments he creates stand on their own as works of design, and that he has even had a show at the prestigious Rhode Island School of Design, Danny acknowledged a contradiction, but remained emphatic that his guitars must never be separated from their musical function.

Rhode Island School of Design show of Ferrington's guitars, 1982

Mike Campbell performing on his double-neck with Tom Petty and the Heartbreakers, 1991

"One of the most important parts of being a guitar maker for me is knowing that my instruments will be making good music long after they are finished," he insisted. While not wishing to downplay the visual qualities of his guitars, Danny admitted that in the last few years he has moved away from some of the flashier instruments he made in the early eighties, which emphasized finishing and inlaying, and toward less showy and simpler designs involving more natural wood finishes. 'What appeals to me now is a cleaner, more elegant look that does not depend so much on ornamentation or color for its visual impact." In fact, he plans to finish the string quartet he has been working on, not in the gaudy colors he once imagined, but in a single, less provocative spectrum of color tones that will begin in a light shade for the violins, and then become increasingly darker for the viola and cello.

By 1992 Ferrington had constructed more than one hundred custom-made guitars, and showed no evidence of having lost his gusto for making another one hundred. In fact he seemed more enamored than ever of this craft that was born in his father's Louisiana bayou cabinet shop twenty-five years ago. It was only after knowing their son for more than a decade that I finally met Loyd and Amy Ferrington. It was only then that I really understood not only how Danny came to be such a magician with wood, but also how he was able to establish such a unique relationship with both his clients and the instruments he made for them. When I saw the way his parents looked at him with a combination of wonder and respect, I realized it was the same look that Danny reserves for his instruments, the look of fond pride that parents reserve for their children.

Amy and Loyd Ferrington, 1991

"What's so nice about my instruments is that they are, in fact, like my children," Danny, who is not yet married, told me. "I have an ongoing relationship with them, and even when I sell them they never completely leave me. They may live at someone else's house, but I feel that somehow they are still mine. I really love to go and visit them to see how they're doing, and when they come back into my shop to get fixed up, it's like they're coming home. But what I love most of all is when I hear the music they make. Sometimes I'll just be driving along the freeway, and suddenly I'll hear one come out of the car radio. Or recently I was in a Hard Rock Cafe and they played almost a solid hour of music that was all made by artists who have my guitars. There was Squeeze, Eric Clapton, Crowded House, Pete Townshend. I just can't tell you how proud and good that made me feel."

Neil
FINN

The folks in Neil's band, Crowded House, are very artistic people who are really close with their families, and for a while everybody in the band wore matching jackets with the names of their family members painted on the lapels like medals on a general's uniform.

Neil wanted to do something similar for the inlays on the fretboard of his guitar, and the two of us decided to use symbols to represent the members of his family alongside their names.

His mother is part Irish, for example, so she's represented by the shamrock.

And his two sisters, who like to dance, are symbolized by the girls dressed in 60s and 70s clothes.

1988 | 25 3/8 inches   *Spruce* top   *mahogany* body and neck   *ebony* fretboard

Originally a member of Split Enz, Neil Finn is the lead singer, songwriter, guitar player, and co-founder of the energetic New Zealand/Australian band Crowded House. Crowded House has gained a reputation as an infectiously spontaneous and entertaining live band, dubbed "the most extraordinary live act in the solar system" by the Times Tribune. In June 1991 Crowded House released its third album Woodface.

Neil Finn played a Ferrington small guitar, built for his son, on "Four Seasons in One Day," "Weather with You," and "She Goes On," off the Crowded House album Woodface (Capitol/EMI, 1991).

It never would have occurred to me to make a red guitar with a green binding—never!—but at the time Neil was into those black-light posters from the 1970s that have a pulsating effect with the bright reds and greens that fight for dominance when they're placed next to each other. He even gave me some color samples that he'd snipped out of a magazine so I'd know exactly what shades to use.

The collaborative process is definitely one of the things I love most about my work. People often ask me to work within some set of parameters that I never would have imagined otherwise, and after tinkering around for a little bit, I often find that I'm really thrilled with what I end up with, in part because I would never have thought of trying out those ideas by myself.

Reeves
GABRELS

•

David Bowie, whose band Reeves is in, played one of the Kramer factory-made guitars I designed on the first Tin Machine album, so Reeves came by the shop to visit a couple of times just after he moved to L.A. for a while.

His wife said that he talked about my custom guitars so much that she finally offered to buy him one as a wedding anniversary gift.

Reeves was just thrilled about that, and a little while later he stopped by again so that we could go through the whole design process. We worked together to pick out the kinds of wood I'd use, and there was this neat-looking body shape that both of us liked a lot, so he asked me to build him a baritone guitar in this configuration even though I'd never tried that before.

Reeves Gabrels is a songwriter
and lead guitar player with the Tin Machine
band, and his aggressive guitar sound synthesizes the
visceral energy of rock, the sophistication of jazz, and
the emotional honesty of blues and country. Gabrels
attended the Berklee School of Music during the late 1970s,
and then remained in Boston to play in several area bands.
In 1988 he began working with David Bowie in an experimental
band that soon evolved into Tin Machine. Tin Machine will release
a live album in late 1992, while Gabrels has also remained active
composing documentary soundtracks for PBS and David Lynch and
Mark Frost Productions, and performing with his Boston-based band,
The Atom Said.

1991 | 29¾ inches
Baritone

Edelman spruce top Brazilian rosewood body mahogany neck ebony fretboard

A few months later, I'd finished most of the guitar, although I hadn't done the inlays yet, and I went down to the studio to talk with Reeves while the Tin Machine band gathered around to listen to a final mix of their latest record. With the din of the record blaring in the background, Reeves told me that he wanted the inlay shapes to be geometric and sculptural rather than really representing anything in particular.

The guys in the band are all real sharp dressers—Reeves definitely has a modern and refined profile, so after listening to him talk for a while I figured out that he really wanted the inlays to look sort of like the forms Brancusi used in his sculpture.

I brought a book of Brancusi's work back to the studio, Reeves picked out some of the pictures he liked best, and I went home to my shop to transpose these shapes onto the inlays. Later on Reeves told me that he saw one of the Brancusi sculptures we'd used for the inlays while he was walking through the Philadelphia Museum of Art, and his first thought was, "Hey, that looks like my guitar!" That's how closely he came to identify with Brancusi.

Elvis
COSTELLO

Although he was closely identified with the British punk and New Wave movement of the late 1970s, Costello's music is actually more noteworthy for its traditional sophistication, craftsmanship, and lyrical depth. Costello's songs often mix emotional sensitivity with sardonic humor or political commentary, while his commitment to musical experimentation has led him to introduce a variety of new styles into his music, including country-and-western and soul.

I first met Elvis when I was living in Nashville, back when everyone still thought of him as an "angry young man."

Elvis was playing a gig in town and a friend of mine helped me get backstage to meet him. I went back there armed with a few guitars, and some slides of others, and the two of us just had a good time together. I was kind of surprised at what a nice guy he turned out to be—we just clicked right off the bat.

I didn't talk with him again until a year later, when I was living in Los Angeles. Elvis had seen a small guitar I'd built for Nick Lowe, and he called from London one day to order one for himself.

He liked that one a lot, and then when he came to L.A. he mentioned that he was also interested in getting a full-size guitar. We met at the hotel, and he told me that he really liked the way a Gibson mandolin looked.

1981   17 inches   Small   *Spruce* top   *maple* body and neck   *ebony* fretboard

We went back and forth on a hotel notepad
a few times, and I suggested
that we could put a scroll
inlay on the body, and
he came up with the
idea of adding a scroll
to the headstock.

The pearl inlay down the fretboard
was a real country-
and-western touch
right out of
Ernest Tubb.

Elvis trusted that
I knew what a
good guitar ought
to sound like,
so the design
process didn't
take much longer than a half-hour or so.

Elvis Costello

After I shipped it to him in England, he called me up to say that he was
so pleased with its proportions that he had
propped it up at one end of his hallway
so that he could look at it from a distance whenever
he walked through his house.

Elvis Costello played the full-size guitar on
"Man Out of Time," off the Elvis Costello and
the Attractions album *Imperial Bedroom*
(Columbia, 1982).

1981 | 25 ⅜ inches   *Spruce* top *maple* body and neck *ebony* fretboard

1981 | 34 inches
Bass

Spruce top, maple body, neck, and fretboard

E.C.

● This bass is the last of Elvis's guitars that I built, so I combined some of the styles of the previous ones into it.

This is actually a fretless bass—what look like frets are really inlaid plastic strips that are flush with the fretboard surface so you can play on those positions and be in tune. Because Elvis is not a bass player, he likes to use this instrument when he's songwriting; since he's not comfortable with it, it prevents him from falling into any familiar melodic patterns— something he might do when playing a guitar.

It's very hard for musicians not to slip into patterns, so many of them will use this technique; whether it be from pianos to guitars or guitars to pianos, they purposely play something different to stay fresh.

Hoyt
AXTON

•

A talented singer, songwriter, and motion picture actor who began his musical career in the late 1950s writing and performing folk music, Hoyt Axton is the son of country songwriter Mae Boren Axton–author of Elvis Presley's "Heartbreak Hotel." Many of Axton's compositions later became icons of contemporary American culture, including Steppenwolf's versions of "The Pusher" and "Snow Blind Friend," as well as Three Dog Night's recording of "Joy to the World." Axton's music has been more heavily oriented toward country sounds since the 1970s, while the 1980s saw him acting in the films The Black Stallion, Gremlins, and Heart Like a Wheel.

Hoyt's guitars have more ornamentation than anybody else's–he's got real cowboy taste, and he just can't have enough decoration. I met with Hoyt to design the big guitar at his mother's house in Nashville. Hoyt was sitting up in bed eating candy while his road manager and members of his band drifted in and out of the room. I was busy sketching while Hoyt talked, and as I doodled he kept looking over my shoulder saying, "Yep! Put more angels over there! More pearl! I want plenty of pearl! Let's make it real shiny!"

•

He told me to put an albino buffalo on the guitar because it was a powerful symbol for Native Americans, and when I was all done, he just loved the fact that I'd made the buffalo anatomically correct.

The small guitar was built after I moved to Los Angeles. Hoyt said he wanted even more angels on this guitar, so I started scattering them all over the body while drawing the design. When I finally got through we counted them all up, and there were sixteen angels all told. Hoyt suddenly started improvising a song called "Sixteen Angels," and we thought it sounded so good that we decided to stop right there.

I remember one time I was watching a documentary special about Woody Guthrie on TV, and toward the end of the show Hoyt was playing my guitar alongside Arlo Guthrie. It made me feel really proud that something I'd built had some sort of link to Woody Guthrie. Every once in a while, something reminds you of the importance of things that you normally take for granted, and experiences like that always teach me just how lucky I am to be doing work that I love so much.

1 9 8 4 | 19 inches

Spruce top *East Indian rosewood* body *mahogany* neck *ebony* fretboard

1979 | 25⅜ inches

Spruce top *maple* body and neck *ebony* fretboard

Roddy
FRAME

Elvis Costello was a fan of
Roddy Frame and his band
Aztec Camera, and Elvis has
even admitted that the songs
Roddy was writing at age
twenty were better than the
ones he was writing at the
same age. Roddy really liked
the big acoustic guitar that
I built for Elvis, and one
time he even appeared on the
British TV show "Top of the Pops"
playing the guitar that has
"Elvis Costello" inlaid down
the fretboard. It was a great
little joke, but a friend of
Roddy's decided to buy him
one of my guitars as a gift.

In the spirit of Roddy's joke,
I inlaid his name in the same
country-and-western style of writing
that I'd used on Elvis's guitar,
while the body is shaped and styled
like one of the old "Mary Ford"
guitars that Gibson made years ago.

1984 | 25⅜ inches   *Spruce* top *koawood* body *mahogany* neck *ebony* fretboard

I made the back and sides out of koawood, and because the guitar that Mary actually played with her husband Les Paul was decorated in gold metal flake, I designed the top of Roddy's guitar to look just like it. All in all, it made for a really good-sounding guitar.

Scottish singer, songwriter, and guitar player Roddy Frame has been making albums since 1981, when he was sixteen years old. Frame's band, Aztec Camera, toured the United States with Elvis Costello in 1983, and helped create a style of intelligent, acoustic guitar-driven rock that remains a mainstay of alternative music. His most recent album was recorded in New York with production assistance by Ryuichi Sakamoto.

Emmylou
HARRIS

After performing as a backup vocalist for Gram Parsons (of the Flying Burrito Brothers) during the first half of the 1970s, Harris ended the decade as an established solo artist. Alternating between country and rock musical styles, Harris brings her sweet soprano voice to all her performances. Her musical collaborations have included sessions with Roy Orbison, Dolly Parton, and Linda Ronstadt, while her recent live album, <u>Emmylou at the Ryman</u>, featured her totally acoustic band, The Nash Ramblers.

1980 | 17 inches   *Spruce* top *maple* body and neck *ebony* fretboard
Small

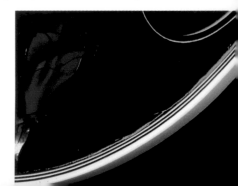

I've known Emmy real well for more than fifteen years, and for years there was just no getting her away from her old Gibson J200 guitar that she liked so much. Back in Nashville I once made a black guitar specifically with her in mind, but when I finally showed it to her she just didn't want to let go of that Gibson.

Waylon Jennings later bought the black guitar as a present for Johnny Cash. And eventually Emmy asked me to refinish her J200 and inlay a red rose made of tinted pearl into the body.

Afterwards she used the guitar on her album covers and a picture of the rose on a backstage pass, and now that guitar is on display in the Country Music Hall of Fame.

This small guitar was a gift that Linda Ronstadt ordered for Emmy's daughter Meghann just after she was born. Of course, I was thinking about Emmy while I was designing it, so I tried to make it look a lot like a mini-version of Emmy's big guitar, complete with a little rosebud instead of a rose.

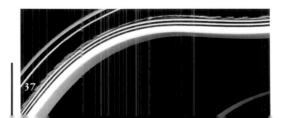

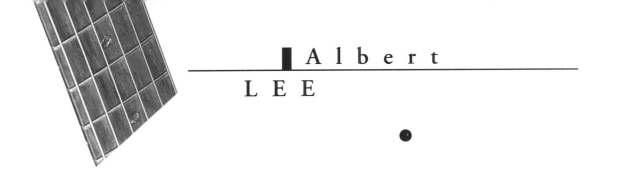

Albert
LEE

●

An active musician since the early 1960s, British guitarist and mandolin player Albert Lee is recognized as one
of the most accomplished country-rock instrumentalists in both Britain and America.
During the 1970s, Lee appeared in a new incarnation of The Crickets, Buddy Holly's original backup band,
before moving on to join Emmylou Harris's Hot Band in 1976. Since 1979 Lee has released several solo albums, while
also contributing to efforts by Jerry Lee Lewis, Eric Clapton, Jackson Browne, and Dave Edmunds.

I built this guitar after the purple prototype that's shown on page 94, which has sort
of a combination X-style bracing pattern and a fan, or classical-style, bracing pattern.
The idea was to help a smaller-body guitar have a louder and more resonant sound.
Since it worked so well on the purple guitar, I wanted to make an even smaller guitar.

Spruce top *maple* body and neck *ebony* fretboard

1989 | 25⅜ inches

I like this guitar because it will fit in an electric guitar case and because of its size,
it's really fun to play. Before Albert owned it, I loaned it out to friends:
Neil Finn used it on the Crowded House *Woodface* album—the band even used it
as a percussion instrument by hitting it on the back with soft mallets—and
David Bowie played it on MTV.

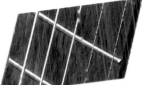

Albert really liked the guitar, so now he has it. I got so used to it being around that it's one of
the few guitars I was sorry to part with. It's really a perfect guitar for him because you can play
it very fast and Albert is definitely one of today's most talented practitioners of real quick,
electric country music playing; his style is influenced by James Burton.
He plays the mandolin real well too, but his electric guitar playing is superlative.

Chris DIFFORD

1981 | 25½ inches

Spruce top *maple* body and neck *ebony* fretboard

Chris Difford is a guitarist, singer, and songwriter with the British band Squeeze. Working in collaboration with fellow band member Glenn Tilbrook, Difford helped develop the distinctively buoyant sound and colorful working-class imagery that characterize Squeeze's music.

Chris saw some of the guitars I'd made for Elvis Costello when his band Squeeze was opening for Elvis during a show, and eventually we got together to collaborate on the designs for two guitars. This small guitar was made to look like an acoustic version of a Rickenbacker-style electric like the kind John Lennon used to play.

It was a little bit tricky to do, because the curves in the points were so sharp that I had to use solid blocks of wood to make the front.
You can't tell what I did when you look at it, though, because I made it appear as if I had actually bent the wood to fit those really sharp angles.

Chris told me to make the finish of the guitar look as if it had just rolled off a factory assembly line, so I let my spray gun splatter a lot while I was painting it. All in all, the guitar has a real 50s style to it, sort of like what you'd expect to see on "American Bandstand." It's just right for Chris.

For the electric, Chris really liked the scroll in the

headstock of Elvis's guitar, except he decided to

take the faux-classical idea to the limit

by making his
electric guitar look exactly
like a violin.

Fender Stratocaster,
which is what
Chris was playing at

I added a
fake F-hole to the
top and a bass

—

the time,
and it's turned out
to be one of |

clef on the back.
The electronics are
just like a

the most
distinctive-looking guitars
I've ever made.

1980 | 25 ⅜ inches *Spruce* top *maple* body and neck *ebony* fretboard

A self-described jack of all trades, in his musical career Nick Lowe has repeatedly alternated between the roles of songwriter, performer, and record producer. During the late 1970s, Lowe's production efforts were reflected in the successful debut recordings of several previously unknown musical talents, including Elvis Costello, the Pretenders, and Graham Parker. Concurrently, Lowe was a member of the band Rockpile along with guitarist Dave Edmunds. Lowe has also recorded several solo albums, although he most recently helped form the band Little Village with Ry Cooder, John Hiatt, and Jim Keltner.

Nick had seen one of my small guitars in England, and a little while later he

called me up to order one. He told me he wanted to use monetary symbols as fretmarkers because he jokingly said he's only in the music business for the money, so I went to the library to make sure that all the international markings would be accurate.

I delivered it to Nick in London, and one night Nick, his then wife Carlene Carter, and I got to talking about this idea I had to build acoustic guitars that were shaped to look like Gibson Explorer electrics.

1980 | 17 inches Small! Spruce top, maple body and neck, ebony fretboard

Both Nick and Carlene thought it was an interesting concept, even though none of us had any idea what an asymmetrical guitar would sound like.

Just after I moved to L.A., Carlene got in touch to say that she wanted me to build the very first Explorer-shaped guitar as a surprise gift for Nick, and to celebrate the occasion, she told me to put a "No. 1" on the headstock and Nick's name on the fretboard. I'd originally designed the guitar for its looks and its style, but when I finished it, we realized that it also had a really great sound.

Nick's guitar validated my theory that asymmetrical guitar designs can actually enhance the sound of the instrument by cutting out a lot of the overtones. A few other people have ordered Explorer-shaped guitars since then, probably because the guitar offers such a comfortable marriage of good looks and good sound.

David
HIDALGO

David Hidalgo played his baritone on "Little John of God," off the Los Lobos album *The Neighborhood* (Slash/Warner Brothers, 1990), and on "Peace," "Shortside of Nothing," and "Kiko and the Lavendar Moon," off the Los Lobos album *Kiko* (Slash/Warner Brothers, 1992).

A member of the East Los Angeles band Los Lobos, Hidalgo is a lead vocalist and songwriter who also plays guitar, fiddle, accordion, lap steel, and percussion. After grounding themselves in traditional Mexican folk music during the late 1970s, the members of Los Lobos moved on to develop a musical style that synthesizes the band's Mexican and Chicano roots with electric guitars and contemporary rock production. The band's 1984 album, <u>How Will the Wolf Survive?</u>, was met with great critical acclaim, and in 1987 Los Lobos recorded the phenomenally successful soundtrack to the Ritchie Valens film biography <u>La Bamba</u>.

I got to know Los Lobos during a telecast of the MTV awards show a few years back. Crowded House was planning to play a few of my guitars during the show, and their dressing room was right next door to the room the Los Lobos guys were using, so I poked my head in and asked if they wanted to see some of my guitars. We talked for a while, and later on I dropped off a few of my guitars for them to experiment with in the studio. David really liked one of the acoustic baritone guitars that I'd made, so he ordered a mahogany baritone to use like a baho sexto, this real deep-sounding Mexican instrument that sounds something like a cross between a bass and a guitar. David gets a real similar tone out of my baritone guitar, so I started calling it an "anglo baho sexto," but because it has such thick strings Dave likes to call it a lap piano.

I've done a whole bunch of little projects for Dave, including putting frets on the fiddle he uses on stage. The frets make it easier for him to keep his fiddle playing in tune while he's swapping between all sorts of different instruments during a gig. At times David has introduced me to people by saying, "This here's Danny Ferrington. He makes lots of weird stuff, but it works!"

1989 | 29¾ inches   *Spruce* top *mahogany* body and neck   *Guatemalan rosewood* fretboard
Baritone

In 1980, Pete's guitar tech, Allen Roagan, helped me get
backstage to see The Who. I carried a few
of my small guitars over to the Boston Garden,
but Pete was still at his hotel, so I just
left them in his dressing room. After the show, the road
manager told me that Pete
wanted me to make two guitars:
one for him and one for his keyboard player,
"Rabbit" Bundrick. He also told me what
colors and what kinds of wood to use.

1980 | 17 inches   *Spruce* top *maple* body and neck *ebony* fretboard
        Small

I didn't actually meet Pete until I visited England a year later. I stopped in at a party
he was holding for the release of his *Empty Glass* album, and there were all these
reporters with microphones and video cameras gathered around him.
I didn't want to interrupt, but it seemed an awful waste to leave England without
saying hello to Pete Townshend. Just before I was ready to go, I leaned across this
table and said, "Excuse me,
but I'm Danny Ferrington, and
I made your little guitar."
Pete just stopped every-
thing, stood up, and said,
"Wait a moment, this is
important!" He thanked
me and said that he really
liked the guitar, and I appreciated the fact
that he gave me those few minutes when he
was obviously so busy with other things.

1989 | 29¾ inches
Baritone

Mahogany top and neck *Sitka spruce* body *Guatemalan rosewood* fretboard

JIMMY
"You're a Hell of a Man" WAYLON

Little Jimmy
DICKENS

A legendary veteran of traditional American country music, Little Jimmy Dickens began his music career playing at a small West Virginia radio station. After he performed with Roy Acuff in Saginaw, Michigan, in 1948, Acuff brought Dickens to Nashville, where he has been a regular performer at the Grand Ole Opry ever since. Little Jimmy Dickens was inducted into the Country Music Hall of Fame in 1983.

Henry heard about my baritone guitars from Richard Thompson, although he didn't play one until we met at a trade show in Anaheim. We stepped into a quiet spot so Henry could try out the baritone in private, and after playing just a few chords he got a real frustrated look on his face and said, "Okay, okay, okay! How much are they?" That was it. Once he came in contact with that baritone, that money was as good as spent. He had to have one.

Henry's music is very experimental and uninhibited. He's got a tremendously exuberant spirit, to the point where he'll meet some interesting musician and practically the third sentence out of his mouth will be "Let's do an album together!" And most of the time, people are so taken by his enthusiasm that they'll end up doing it. The baritone I made for him is pretty straightforward, but when you put Henry into the soup it's a completely different instrument. He gets sounds out of that baritone that nobody else could even begin to imitate.

A resident of the San Francisco Bay area, Kaiser is an adventurous guitarist and songwriter whose highly individualistic style draws from an uncommon range of influences, including traditional blues, North Indian and Hawaiian music, free jazz, free improvisation, and twentieth-century classical music. Kaiser has performed with a similarly diverse group of artists, such as Herbie Hancock, Richard Thompson, Bob Weir, Ryuichi Sakamoto, the ROVA Sax Quartet, and the Golden Palominos.

1980 | 25 3/8 inches
Spruce top *maple* body and neck *ebony* fretboard

Little Jimmy Dickens
is one of the honky-tonk pioneers of country music who
I listened to when I was growing up. Waylon Jennings loaned
Little Jimmy the guitar I'd built for him while they were at the Grand Ole Opry, and later on
I heard that Little Jimmy said, "Now that's a good guitar!" after playing it. Waylon admired Little Jimmy,
so after the gig, he called to order a guitar as a gift for him. Waylon told me to make it exactly like his guitar,
but to inlay a little banner on it saying, "Jimmy, You're a hell of a man!–Waylon."

1989 | 29¾ inches
Baritone electric
Maple top and fretboard *basswood* body and neck

Mike Campbell played his baritone on "King of the Hill," off the Roger McGuinn album *Back from Rio* (Arista, 1991), and on "King's Highway" and "Making Some Noise," off the Tom Petty and the Heartbreakers album *Into the Great Wide Open* (Gone Gator, 1991).

Mike Campbell has been playing lead guitar with Tom Petty since 1969, although the two didn't form the group that would be known as Tom Petty and the Heartbreakers until 1976. In addition to the work he has done with the Heartbreakers, Campbell has contributed his songwriting and guitar-playing talents to songs recorded by Lone Justice, Stevie Nicks, and Don Henley.

Mike's a great guitar player who has really developed his own sound and style. The single-neck baritone electric was the first guitar I ever made for him. It looks like a solid-body, but it's actually semi-acoustic.

The shape of the guitar is derived from the outline of a 1950s Mosrite that looks as if it was made upside-down. Mosrites are so old-fashioned that they've gotten to be kind of cool. Mike's been pretty happy with this guitar, and he's used it while recording a bunch of the albums he's done with Tom Petty and the Heartbreakers.

1991 | 29¾ inches
Double-neck electric

Mahogany top and neck *basswood* body *Brazilian rosewood* fretboard

Mike played almost all the guitar tracks for the band's *Into the Great Wide Open* album, so when the Heartbreakers were getting ready to go out on tour in 1991, he was afraid he'd have to keep changing guitars in the middle of a song in order to duplicate the studio sound while playing live. He wanted a double-neck electric guitar so that he could quickly jump back and forth between a twelve string and a six string while on stage. Lots of companies made double-neck guitars back in the 1950s, so the idea was nothing new, but the problem is that they're awfully heavy—it's almost as if you're wearing two guitars around your neck at once. When I built this guitar, I hollowed out the inside of the body, so it's actually a lot lighter than it looks. Mike's figured out that he can play one neck with the pickup turned off while leaving the pickup for the other neck turned on so that the second pickup catches the sound of his playing sympathetically. It creates a real distant, echoing sound, sort of like somebody playing guitar down at the end of a long hallway.

Mike was using the double-neck almost before the glue had dried and the lacquer had set: barely two hours after it left my hands he was using it to record in the studio. That's one of the best things about doing my kind of work in Los Angeles. To make a guitar that will be fed right into the arteries of the music business is just one of the greatest feelings in the world.

Rosanne
CASH

•

I've built so many guitars for the Cash
family that June Carter Cash once called
me an honorary member of the family.
I made a guitar for Rosanne before I'd
ever even met her, because her father,
Johnny Cash, ordered one for her as a
birthday present real early on. I introduced
myself to Rosanne a few years later and we
got along just fine. Rosanne was married
to Rodney Crowell then, and he decided to
give Rosanne another gift–this time one of
my small guitars. She didn't get to see
either one of the guitars before she received
them, but Johnny'd told me, back when he
ordered her full-size, that Rosanne really
liked rusty colors. The small guitar has
Rosanne's name inlaid in it, along with the
same kind of star pattern inlay on the
fretboard that I'd used when making her big
guitar. The Cash family is such a nice,
down-to-earth bunch of folks that it's always
a real pleasure to make guitars for them.

*Singer, songwriter, and daughter of
country music artist Johnny Cash,
Rosanne embraces in her music both
traditional Nashville sounds and
California country-rock, and she has
found success with fans of both
musical styles. In 1991 Rosanne
toured Australia with
Mary-Chapin Carpenter
and Lucinda Willams, and
she expects to release a new
album, co-produced with
John Leventhal, in
late 1992.*

1981 17 inches Small Spruce top *maple* body and neck *ebony* fretboard

1979 | 25⅜ inches   *Spruce* top and body, *maple* neck, *ebony* fretboard

Phoebe SNOW

Rodney CROWELL

A versatile country-
rock singer, songwriter,
and record producer, Crowell
was a member of Emmylou Harris's
Hot Band touring group until 1977.
During the early 1980s Crowell's prolific
songwriting yielded compositions that were
popularized by musicians such as Crystal Gayle, Bob Seger,
and Waylon Jennings, while the latter half of the decade witnessed
his emergence as a successful solo artist. His 1988 _Diamonds and Dirt_
album produced five number one singles–a first in country music history.
His latest album is entitled _Life Is Messy_.

Phoebe Snow is a singer, songwriter, and guitarist noted for her superb voice and remarkable versatility. Growing up in New York City during the late 1950s and early 1960s, Phoebe was influenced early on by the music of Woody Guthrie, Leadbelly, Mississippi John Hurt, Mahalia Jackson, and Aretha Franklin. After beginning her singing career in New York's Greenwich Village, Snow released her first album in 1974. Her later recordings have seen her experimenting with folk, rock, and jazz, although her forthcoming release, produced by Nile Rogers, will have a strong rhythm-and-blues sound.

1980 | 17 inches
Small

Spruce top East Indian rosewood body mahogany neck ebony fretboard

Musicians usually respond to my little guitars in the same way that people react when they see a little baby's fingers: Their voice goes up real high and they'll say something like, "Oh, look! It even has little tuners!" The small guitars seem kind of warm and comfortable to them, just like a little baby. But after most professionals pick one up and start playing, they realize it's not a toy; it's a different voice.

This guitar is a lot like Linda Ronstadt's, which Phoebe had tried out while Linda was living in New York to do *The Pirates of Penzance*. Phoebe's guitar has a lot less ornamentation than Linda's, and after I gave it to her, she put a big picture of it on the back cover of her *Rock Away* album along with a little footnote thanking me for building the baby guitar. Gestures like that are a lot of fun, mainly because they help remind me that my guitars have a positive impact upon the people who use them.

When Rodney and I sat down together to design his guitar, we spent a long time talking while I tried to figure out exactly what kind of guitar he wanted me to make. I kept throwing out ideas and describing some of the guitars I'd built for other people, and Rodney kept commenting on how unique my work was. After we'd been doing this for a while, Rodney finally just broke into a big smile and said, "Danny, you're a guitartist!"

Rodney really likes the Gibson J45 guitar, so the guitar I made is styled like a shrunk-down version of the Gibson. For a songwriter like Rodney, a little guitar is a fun thing to have because it's very portable and the sound is so different that it helps him to develop new musical ideas.

1980 | 17 inches   *Spruce* top *maple* body and neck *ebony* fretboard
Small

1. The shape of the guitar is designed, then drawn on construction paper and cut out to make a pattern.

2. To construct the body of the guitar, a form (or template) is built. Danny makes his form from scraps of wood that are glued and then clamped together into a solid mass. The form is then cut into the pattern's shape with a band saw.

3. Woods are joined for the top (or soundboard) and back. The edges to be joined are first sanded smooth, and then glued together and tied into an old-fashioned rope clamp, so the joint will be even and secure. This guitar will have a spruce top and a mahogany back.

4. The top and back are cut out with a
   band saw according to the pattern;
   the inside surfaces are sanded smooth.

5. Reinforcement braces,
   made from strips
   of quarter-sawn spruce,
   are glued onto the
   insides of the top and
   back and clamped
   into position.

The top braces are
hand-shaped with
a chisel.

The inside top of
the guitar is signed
and dated.

Danny uses a variety of patterns to brace the tops of his guitars;
for this one he is using a standard X-pattern. The braces on the top must be light, yet strong,
so the top will vibrate like a diaphragm, moving in and out.
The braces, or struts, on the back are
designed primarily for strength, but they must also be arched to give a parabolic
shape to the back, so the sound will project
out of the soundhole. Because the way the braces are
patterned and shaped can radically affect the sound of the guitar,
this is a crucial step.

6. The wood for the sides (in this case mahogany)
   is soaked in water for hours, to make it pliable;
   then it is bent and shaped over a heated
   iron pipe. Sides are then clamped into the form
   and left overnight to dry.

7. To hold the sides together, top and bottom end blocks are glued and clamped in place. The top block is larger because the neck will be joined to the body at this point.

8. The neck is cut from a piece of mahogany, and a slot is routed along the length of the neck for an adjustable steel truss rod; the truss rod is installed into the slot, and a strip of wood is glued and clamped into position over it. The truss rod adds strength to the neck, and its tension can be adjusted by turning a nut when switching to different-gauge strings. The adjusting nut is located in a cavity below the surface of the headstock that Danny will later conceal with a small wooden truss rod cover.

9. A pattern is made for the headstock.

10. **Constructing the fretboard (made of Brazilian rosewood):**

a. The scale of the fretboard is marked.

b. Slots are cut with a fret saw to accommodate the fretwire.

c. Position markers are cut out from thin mother-of-pearl with a jeweler's saw

d. A small router cuts the holes for the pearl.

e. The pearl is glued into the holes. Because the holes are oversized, Danny uses a paste, mixed from matching wood dust and epoxy, to fill in the cracks. After the paste dries, he will sand the pearl smooth to reveal a perfect inlay.

f. The fretwire is hammered into the slots. After the guitar has been lacquered, Danny will go back and level the fretwire surfaces with a flat file, and then re-round them with a concave file.

11. The finished fretboard is glued and clamped to the front of the neck.

12. The position of the headstock veneer, cut out according to the pattern, is marked; headstock veneer is glued and clamped onto the top of the neck.

13. The neck is shaped and sanded smooth with a variety of rasps and files until it becomes smooth enough to use sandpaper. This is very physical work, as Danny does it all by hand.

14. To provide a joining surface for the top and back, a kerfing strip (or lining) is glued along the inside edges of the sides and clamped in place with clothespins. To aid in bending the strip, saw cuts are made through the bulk of the lining at quarter- or half-inch intervals.

15. First the top and then the back are glued onto the sides and clamped into position.

16. The body is sanded smooth, and a ledge is
routed along the outside edges, where the top
and back join the sides, for the binding trim;
binding is glued into the ledge and filed level.

17. The mother-
of-pearl logo is
inlaid at the top of
the headstock.

18. The nut is glued into a slot located at
the point where the headstock joins the
beginning of the fretboard. The nut is a piece
of bone (never ivory), or wood, with slots cut
into it for the strings to sit in.

19. The neck is joined to the body of the guitar. To join the neck,
an approximately half-inch recess, or pocket, has been cut through the top
of the guitar and the top end block. However, Danny will not bolt the
neck to the body until both have been finished with lacquer.
Danny builds bolt-on necks for his acoustics, just like the necks
on some electric guitars.

20. Here Danny is
positioning the bridge,
made from Brazilian
rosewood, which will be
attached after the
guitar has been
lacquered. Before the
bridge is attached,
Danny will drill holes
into it for the strings
to pass through
(the strings have brass
balls at the ends to
anchor them), and cut
an angle slot for the
bone saddle to fit into.

Danny will complete a few additional steps
(not pictured) before the guitar is finished.
To prepare for the guitar to be lacquered,
Danny sands the body and neck with
different-grit sandpapers, from 50 grit down
to the finest 220 grit. When they are both
smooth enough, the lacquer finish is applied.
This guitar has a very thin matte finish.

After the finish is dry, the neck is bolted on with long screws,
from either the front or the back; the truss rod cover is attached;
the bridge is glued into place (see 20); and the frets are dressed
(see 10f). Finally, holes are drilled into the headstock for the
tuners to be bolted on and then the guitar is strung.
And there you have it—a Ferrington-made guitar.

R i c h a r d
THOMPSON

The very first time I heard Richard Thompson play, I was so impressed with his style that I thought, "Hey, I'd really like to make him a guitar." That was just before the show at the Rhode Island School of Design, so I offered to trade him a guitar if he'd play at the opening. We worked it out so that the date of my opening coincided with a time when Richard was going to be near Providence, and I set to work making him a black acoustic guitar. The point in the upper left is like the kind you'd find on a mandolin, and Richard likes the sound of mahogany so much that we decided to use that kind of wood throughout the guitar.

British singer, songwriter, and guitar player Richard Thompson co-founded the British folk-rock band Fairport Convention in 1967. Since beginning a solo career in 1971, Thompson has integrated his remarkable guitar-playing ability and deep singing voice into a unique style of music that creatively combines the themes and cadences of traditional Olde English music with contemporary rock sensibilities. His most recent album, a collection of fourteen songs that are by turns haunting and hilarious, is entitled _Rumor and Sigh_.

Spruce top *mahogany* body and neck *ebony* fretboard

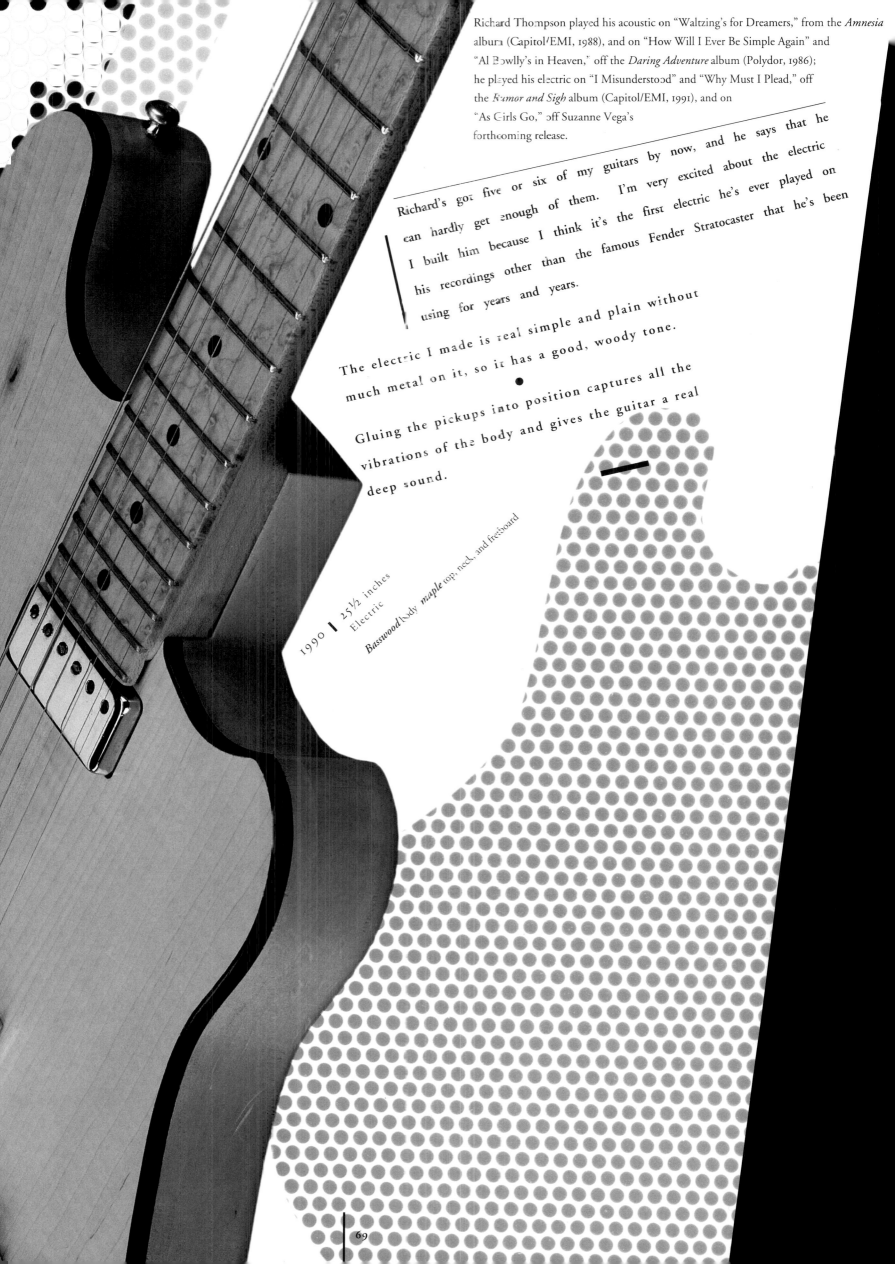

Richard Thompson played his acoustic on "Waltzing's for Dreamers," from the *Amnesia* album (Capitol/EMI, 1988), and on "How Will I Ever Be Simple Again" and "Al Bowlly's in Heaven," off the *Daring Adventure* album (Polydor, 1986); he played his electric on "I Misunderstood" and "Why Must I Plead," off the *Rumor and Sigh* album (Capitol/EMI, 1991), and on "As Girls Go," off Suzanne Vega's forthcoming release.

Richard's got five or six of my guitars by now, and he says that he can hardly get enough of them. I'm very excited about the electric I built him because I think it's the first electric he's ever played on his recordings other than the famous Fender Stratocaster that he's been using for years and years.

The electric I made is real simple and plain without much metal on it, so it has a good, woody tone.

Gluing the pickups into position captures all the vibrations of the body and gives the guitar a real deep sound.

1990 | 25½ inches
Electric
Basswood body *maple* top, neck, and fretboard

Stephen wanted a full-size acoustic guitar, and when it came time to choose the colors for the body and binding, Stephen brought a pair of pink socks and a baby blue shirt down to my shop and told me to use those two colors on the guitar.

Stephen is pretty well known for dressing in real bold, colorful clothes—plaids, on top of polka dots, on top of stripes—so I guess it makes sense that he decided to look through his closets while deciding what colors to use on the guitar.

•

Singer-songwriter Stephen Bishop's gentle ballads about love and life have included such successful songs as "On and On" and "Separate Lives" (recorded by Phil Collins). He has also contributed to several motion pictures, including playing a small but memorable role in _Animal House_, which featured Bishop singing a song entitled "I Gave My Love a Cherry." He also performed the theme song for the movie _Tootsie_. Bishop plans to complete a South American tour during the summer of 1992, with a new album release expected shortly thereafter.

•

The inlays down the
fretboard all represent some
aspect of Stephen's life.

The clarinet was the first
instrument he ever played,
and the profile of himself is a
little thing he used to draw in
high school.

•

The thing that looks like a
sunburst is another doodle,
and Stephen says that it's a
symbolic representation of his
creative process.

•

Space Invaders was a video
game Stephen liked to play
back when I built the guitar,
and the mailbox with the
street address commemorates
the first place where he ever
wrote a song.

•

Sinatra and the Beatles made
it onto the fretboard because
they were Stephen's two
biggest influences early on,
and the bed with the guitar
leaning up against it recalls a
song he wrote called "Sleeping
with Girls."

It's a real photogenic guitar, so Stephen has used it on his album covers and on TV a whole bunch of times. It's obviously a bright and wacky guitar, and that makes it just right for him!

THE BEATLES

1984 | 25⅜ inches

Spruce top *maple* body and neck *ebony* fretboard

Jackson
BROWNE

When I first moved to L.A. I carried around a whole set of slides in my car so that I could show people pictures of the custom guitars I'd built no matter where I happened to be. Jackson liked the Explorer-shaped guitar in one of the slides because he was interested in unusual guitars and had picked up a bunch of old ones over the years. He liked the way the Explorer was shaped, but he wanted something real thin—like an electric—because he thought the sound would come out more quickly that way.

I told him I'd give it a try, even though I'd never made a thin acoustic guitar before. I'd built a few that were shaped like electrics, but I'd never gone all the way to make them thin like an electric.

It turned out to be a good idea because this guitar has a completely unique character and personality. It has more of an immediate presence to it and a less resonant sound. Musicians are always hoping to find instruments with a different sound because it helps them evoke new melodies or new songs: it's sort of like putting on a new shirt. You just get tired of seeing yourself in the same clothes all the time, and every once in a while you want to try something a little different.

Jackson Browne's career as a singer and songwriter began when several of his early compositions were recorded by artists such as Linda Ronstadt, Bonnie Raitt, and The Byrds. During the 1970s Browne established himself as an influential spokesman for the Los Angeles country-rock sound, and his songs during this period often expressed introverted and deeply personal emotional themes. Since 1979, when Browne helped organize the MUSE (Musicians United for Safe Energy) concerts at New York's Madison Square Garden, much of his work has contained a strong undercurrent of social commentary and political activism.

1981 | 25⅜ inches | Maple top and neck Sitka spruce body ebony fretboard

Kurt Cobain is lead singer and guitarist for the Seattle-based rock trio Nirvana, whose 1991 album, Nevermind, catapulted the group to superstar status virtually overnight. Nirvana's music has strong antecedents in the British punk rock movement of the late 1970s, combining hard-driving melodies with Cobain's urgent vocals and lyrics that are unpretentiously insightful and often bitterly ironic.

1992 | 24 inches
Electric

Basswood body maple neck Brazilian rosewood fretboard

Kurt is left-handed, and he really likes the Fender Mustang he's been playing for a few years. But his playing style is so rough, and left-handed Mustangs so rare, that it was beginning to look as if his favorite guitar was going to break apart right out from under him. I'd talked with Nick Close, one of Nirvana's roadies, about trying to find replacement necks for the Mustang, but finally Kurt called me to talk about ordering a new custom guitar.

Nirvana left for Australia a few days later, and Kurt faxed me a great little picture showing where he wanted the pickups to be and what shape to use for the body. It was the first time I'd collaborated by fax, and I thought it was real fun to be designing a guitar by long distance using such a modern communications technology.

I built his guitar to be a lot like that old Mustang, except we used a Gibson-style bridge that's better at keeping the guitar in tune, and I made the neck a little straighter so that it won't be so apt to break when Kurt plays it hard. It's tricky making left-handed guitars, though, because everything on a left-handed guitar is counter-intuitive for me. Right off the bat I made a few mistakes on Kurt's guitar, so finally I took to labeling all the parts "This Side Up" to remind myself that I needed to do everything backwards.

The guitar turned out real well, and a few months later Kurt came by with his wife to pick it up. Just after he started playing it he stopped dead in his tracks and said, "This is like my dream guitar!" His wife asked, "Honey, are you gonna trash this one too?" but Kurt got this horrified look on his face, and in a solemn voice he said, "No, this one's going to be my recording guitar." I was tickled to death, and it was incredibly satisfying to hear that I'd hit the nail right on the head.

•

Don
WAS

*Don Was is a bass player, songwriter, and record producer.
He currently performs with his band Was (Not Was), a virtuoso group
that often mixes the musical styles of funk and soul with humorous or
surreal lyrics. Was gained substantial recognition after producing
Bonnie Raitt's Grammy-winning Nick of Time album, and his other
production credits include collaborations with Bob Dylan, Elton John,
Iggy Pop, Paula Abdul, The B-52's, Israeli female vocalist Ofra Haza, and
Algerian Raï music artist Cheb Khaled.*

I really admired the work Don did with his band Was (Not Was), but I didn't get to know him until we were introduced at a BMI awards dinner. When Don and I started talking, he mentioned that he wanted to get one of my basses. I loaned him a few of my bass guitars for a while, and then later he asked if I would make him one with wooden frets that would cut out the metallic "clack" you sometimes hear when the strings hit the frets.

Nobody had ever suggested using wooden frets before, so I was definitely willing to give it a try. When I was done, the guitar had a very quiet sound–much like a fretless bass–and bass players always tell me that the fretboard has a real warm feel to it.

The shape of the body is designed so that there's more top surface on the bass side of the strings to accentuate the bass notes, while the treble side is tapered off to help bring out the highs. I think it gives the guitar a more resonant, balanced sound. Don asked me to make the guitar look like it was real old by putting fake cigarette burns on it, giving it a few dings, and rubbing most of the finish off, but it pained me too much to actually do it because I felt that it was about as good a piece of woodworking as I'd ever done. Maybe after some time I won't mind going back to trash it out, but I figure that before too long it will end up looking old in its natural way.

1991 | 34 inches
Bass

Spruce top *mahogany* body and neck *ebony* fretboard

Michael
ANTHONY

Bass player Michael Anthony was born in Chicago, Illinois, but moved to the Los Angeles area as a child. After playing in several high school rock-and-roll bands, he became a founding member of the heavy metal band Van Halen in 1974. Van Halen found early commercial success during the late 1970s, and the band's popularity expanded steadily throughout the 1980s. Van Halen's 1991 release was entitled _For Unlawful Carnal Knowledge_.

Spruce top *maple* body and neck *ebony* fretboard

Mike also told me to
make it with tons of
flames all along the top
because he's a real car
enthusiast and he
wanted his bass to look
like one of those old hot
rods from the 1950s.
When I was done
building the guitar, you
could almost guess right
away that it belonged to
somebody in a band
like Van Halen.
Those flames are
really fun, and
they make
the guitar
look so
hot!

After I finished
building my very first
acoustic bass,
I took it around town
to show people and get
their opinions about it.
Mike liked the proto-
type so much that he
played it while recording
a song called "Big Bad
Bill and Sweet William
Now" off Van Halen's
Diver Down album.
When it came time to
order one, though, he
wanted me to make
one with both an
electric pickup
and an acoustic-
style pickup.

Carlene
CARTER

●

1980 | 25⅜ inches

Spruce top *maple* body and neck *ebony* fretboard

Carlene knew me even before we'd ever met because I'd made her mom, June Carter Cash, a guitar a few years before. We got to know each other pretty well while I was living in Nashville, and later on, after Carlene gave Nick Lowe my first Explorer-shaped guitar as a gift, she decided that she wanted a bright red one for herself too. Apart from the inlay of her initials that I put on the fretboard, I also put a "No. 2" on the headstock since hers was the second Explorer I built.

I also ordered a special case for Carlene's guitar with fake snow leopard fur lining the inside. It practically makes you jump when you open up that case and see the bright red guitar surrounded by all this spotted fur staring right at you—folks just love it.

●

Carlene Carter is a third-generation member of the famous Carter family—the founders of modern country music. Although steeped in country styles, Carlene gravitated toward rock-and-roll during the 1980s. Her connection to the Nashville music scene has always remained strong, however, and Carlene's more recent efforts have returned her to a more traditional country sound. Her 1990 release I Fell in Love was followed by a busy touring schedule, and her newest album is planned for release in the fall of 1992.

I once saw Carlene playing on The Nashville Network with her sisters, and it just killed me to see her out there playing this real wild, red guitar while on stage with the family that practically invented traditional country music. But she's always been the rock-and-roll rebel in the family, so the juxtaposition seemed right on to me.

John
PRINE

Michael decided to buy an electric baritone, and he came to my shop to design it with me. It's got a humbucking pickup in the back position, and the neck goes into the body a lot to help hide the added length of the baritone neck.

1992 ■ 27/8 inches *Mahogany* body and neck *Brazilian rosewood* fretboard
Baritone electric

Michael told me to use little representations of a femur bone for the position markers down the fretboard because he really likes "The Flintstones," and up on stage he sometimes uses a plastic femur bone to strum his guitar. It's a joke, of course, but he also likes the distorted sound he gets when he draws that fake bone across the strings.

•

*Renowned for her
extremely natural-sounding
yet well-controlled voice,
Ronstadt began her career
with the Southern California
band the Stone Poneys
in the late 1960s. After
finding extraordinary
success performing country
and rock music during the
1970s, Ronstadt appeared
in New York in the
Broadway production of
Gilbert and Sullivan's
The Pirates of Penzance
in 1981, and in 1984
she performed as Mimi in
Puccini's opera La Bohème.
Her album releases during
the 1980s experimented
with ballads from the
big band era, traditional
country music, and
Mexican folk singing.
Linda's newest album of
mambo music is planned for
release in the fall of 1992.*

When I was in
Nashville I used
to do a lot of
guitar repairs for
the guys in
Crystal's band, so I got to know her
while hanging
out during their
rehearsals and
gigs. She heard
about my small
guitars and asked
to see one of them, so I stopped by
her office one day
and she ordered
one in the same
color as the red
Mercedes she was
driving at the time.

She also wanted
me to put her
name in it, so I
made a copy of
the signature that
she had used as a
logo on one of
her album covers and inlaid it on
the front in pearl.
This guitar was
one of the last
things I made
before I finally left
Nashville to move
to L.A.

John David
SOUTHER

1982 | 24½ inches   *Spruce* top *maple* body and neck *ebony* fretboard

J. D.'s a big fan of Gibson "Everly Brothers" guitars, so we started with that basic size before I gave it an asymmetrical shape. It's made of maple, so it turned out to be a real warm, rich-sounding guitar–J. D. likes to use it while playing his slow ballads because it's got such a beautiful tone.

It was J. D.'s idea to include Texas in the design, and he told me that if we were going to do it, he wanted to do it right.

A few days later I picked up a Texas state map that he'd pulled out of some book, and eventually we worked out the idea of putting the top half of the state on the headstock and the bottom half down by the end of the fretboard.

Originally from Texas, John David Souther is a guitarist, singer, and songwriter whose country-rock ballads have been recorded by artists such as Linda Ronstadt, Bonnie Raitt, and Clint Black. Souther has also collaborated extensively with Don Henley, co-writing some of the most memorable Eagles songs, including "Heartache Tonight" and "New Kid in Town"; the duo achieved success again in 1991 with Henley's recording of "Heart of the Matter." In 1983 Souther released a highly successful solo album entitled You're Only Lonely, and he has recently been working with Heart on its forthcoming album. He is currently in the process of starting his own cattle ranch.

Now J. D. likes to say that every note he plays is in the state of Texas. He also wanted me to inlay a little star in the headstock to mark Amarillo, the town where he grew up. J. D. was good friends with Roy Orbison, and Roy just loved J. D.'s guitar because he was from Vernon, Texas. But J. D. told me that every time Roy saw that guitar he would say, "J. D., that star is in the wrong place!" Everybody who's from Texas seems to fall for J. D.'s guitar, and he usually wears it around as if it was a trophy.

Purple
PROTOTYPE

•

The Purple Prototype

was the product

of an idea I had

after thinking about the playing style of

Dweezil Zappa. Dweezil has a few of my guitars, and he's

a real fast guitar player, but folks like him don't usually use

acoustic guitars because the strings are so heavy that it's

practically impossible to play in the kind of quick,

pyrotechnical style that they like so much. Musicians occasionally

try to compensate by putting electric strings on an acoustic guitar, but the sound

ends up being so soft that it's sometimes hard to hear what's being played.

I thought I'd try using a very light bracing pattern across the top of an acoustic guitar so the instrument would have a regular acoustic presence even though it's strung with electric guitar strings.

1987 | 25½ inches   *Spruce* top **maple** body and neck ***ebony*** fretboard

The Purple Prototype allows musicians like Dweezil to transpose their electric technique onto an acoustic guitar without having to make any adjustments in playing style, and the sound that they get on my guitar is unique.

R y
C O O D E R

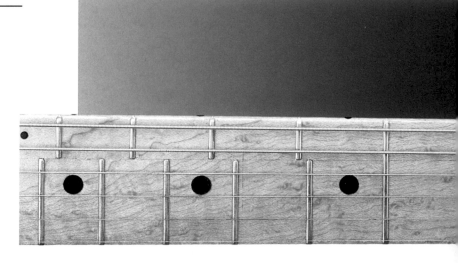

A singer, songwriter, and virtuoso on most fretted instruments, Cooder embraces traditional blues, gospel, country-and-western, calypso, avant-garde rock, and jazz. Cooder started his career by collaborating with Taj Mahal, Captain Beefheart, and the Rolling Stones in the 1960s, but after 1970 he established himself as a solo artist of exceptional talent and versatility. Cooder has also composed several motion picture scores, including the highly atmospheric soundtrack to *Paris, Texas*. More recently, Cooder has appeared with Nick Lowe, John Hiatt, and Jim Keltner in a band called Little Village.

Ry Cooder has an amazing ear for tone and is extremely particular about the guitars he'll play. So I was really pleased when Kenny Edwards told me that Ry had played one of my acoustic basses and declared it to be "a useable instrument." Coming from Ry, those words were high praise.

Since then, Ry has bought four or five of my guitars, and because he lives along the route I take to get from my house to my workshop, he's one of the people I look to for input when I'm trying out a new guitar. I call him my "roadtester."

1988 | 29¾ inches
Baritone

Spruce top **mahogany** body and neck **Guatemalan rosewood** fretboard

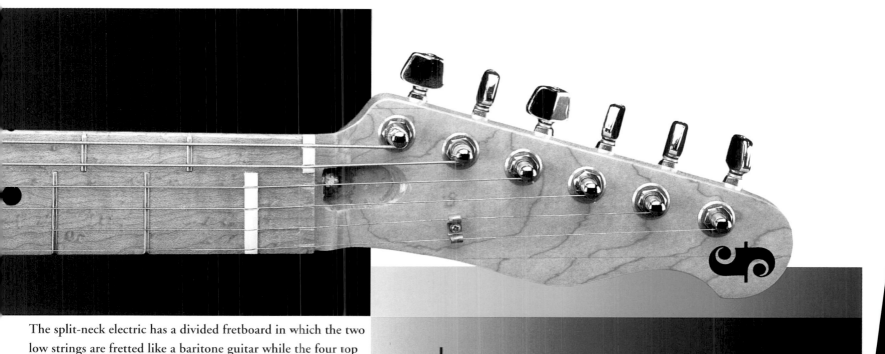

The split-neck electric has a divided fretboard in which the two low strings are fretted like a baritone guitar while the four top strings are on a regular electric scale. Ry has his own tuning for it, and he's one of the only people I know of who can play that guitar. He's used it all over the Little Village album.

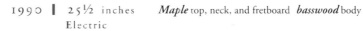

1990 | 25½ inches *Maple* top, neck, and fretboard *basswood* body
Electric

The baritone acoustic guitar is one of the first baritones I ever made, and Ry makes it sound like a big old twelve-string, like the one Leadbelly used. I copied the scale off one of Ry's old electric guitars, because he told me that that particular guitar had a good scale for a baritone. I've used that same scale on all my baritones ever since.

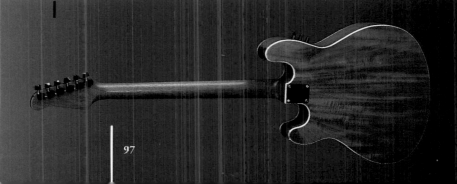

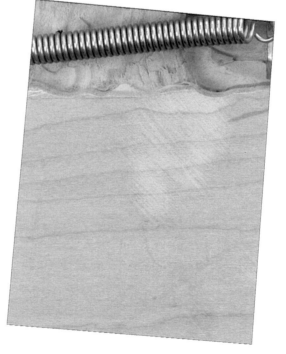

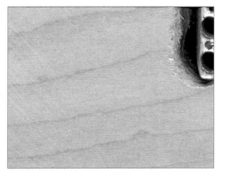

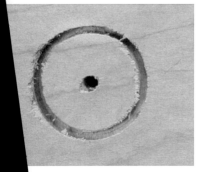

Ry Cooder played the one-hour guitar
on "Let Me Go Back to the Country,"
off the Bobby and Terry album *Live
and Let Live* (Rounder Records, 1988).

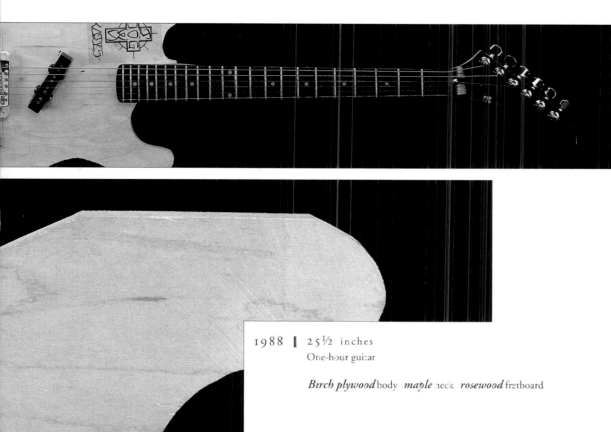

1988 | 25½ inches
One-hour guitar

Birch plywood body *maple* neck *rosewood* fretboard

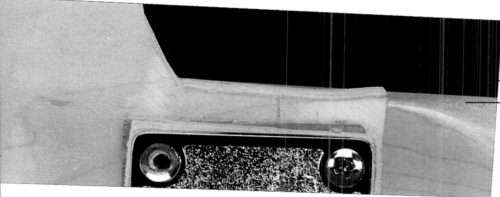

Ry is good at taking whatever he's given and finding some way to use it. The liking he took to my plywood "one-hour guitar" is typical of his love of the unusual. I'd built that guitar just to test out this Fender jazz bass pickup that I'd found, and when I was done I thought it had a great sound, sort of like something being played underwater. I also showed him an electric guitar that I built for myself and Ry said, while playing it, "Danny, I can't let you leave with this guitar." I had to leave it at his house, and he's used it on a couple of his records. Nowadays I'm more careful about what I take over to Ry's because I know that whatever I show him might not come home with me again.

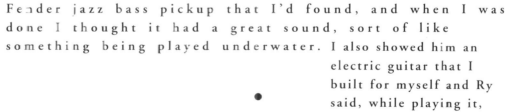

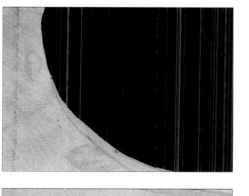

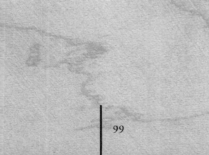

Michael
LANDAU

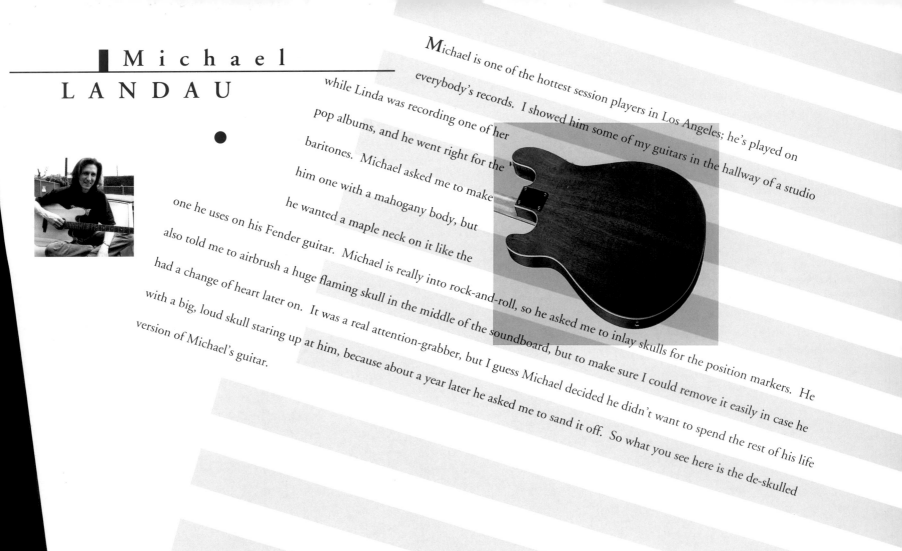

Michael is one of the hottest session players in Los Angeles; he's played on everybody's records. I showed him some of my guitars in the hallway of a studio while Linda was recording one of her pop albums, and he went right for the baritones. Michael asked me to make him one with a mahogany body, but he wanted a maple neck on it like the one he uses on his Fender guitar. Michael is really into rock-and-roll, so he asked me to inlay skulls for the position markers. He also told me to airbrush a huge flaming skull in the middle of the soundboard, but to make sure I could remove it easily in case he had a change of heart later on. It was a real attention-grabber, but I guess Michael decided he didn't want to spend the rest of his life with a big, loud skull staring up at him, because about a year later he asked me to sand it off. So what you see here is the de-skulled version of Michael's guitar.

1988 | 29¾ inches
Baritone

Spruce top   *mahogany* body   *maple* neck   *rosewood* fretboard

A highly sought-after Los Angeles guitarist, Landau gravitates toward blues-rock, although he can perform almost any style of music gracefully and proficiently. Landau has performed on albums with Joni Mitchell, Rod Stewart, and Miles Davis, and he has also been a member of James Taylor's touring band. Landau is currently a member of a psychedelic blues-rock band called Burning Water.

Randy plays with Don Was in a band called Was (Not Was), and for a while I let Don borrow one of my baritone electric guitars. Randy saw it lying around Don's house and took to playing it once in a while. We talked about designing a guitar for him, but then, when Christmas started to roll around, Don decided to buy the baritone for Randy as a gift.

Randy
JACOBS

While he was learning to play guitar in Detroit, Randy Jacobs's musical influences included the sounds of Wes Montgomery, Led Zeppelin, country music, and traditional R&B and his musical career has seen him performing with a similarly diverse group of musicians. Jacobs played in a variety of R&B bands during the 1970s before collaborating with Michael Henderson, Miles Davis's bass player, during 1978 and 1979. Since he became a founding member of Was (Not Was) in 1981, Jacobs's performance credits have included collaborations with B. B. King, Roy Orbison, Bonnie Raitt, and Iggy Pop.

The baritone is just right for Randy because he's got a finger-picking style that allows him to play the bass lines with his thumb while picking the other notes with his fingers. The baritone has such a low register on the bass notes that when Randy uses this guitar, it really sounds like two people playing two different instruments. He's gotten really attached to the baritone and it's indicative of the way musicians usually feel about their instruments that he called me a few days after I borrowed the guitar for the photo shoot to say, "Hey, Danny, where's my baby?"

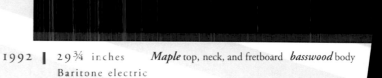

1992 | 29¾ inches   *Maple* top, neck, and fretboard *basswood* body
Baritone electric

Jamie
SOLOW

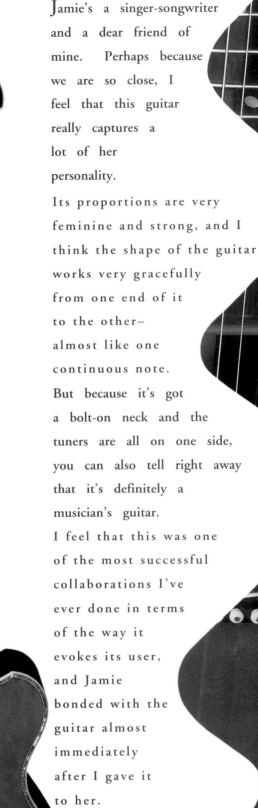

Jamie Solow is a Los Angeles-based singer and songwriter who also works as a child therapist. Her early musical influences included jazz and classical music as well as the recordings of Tom Waits and Taj Mahal, and her evocative songs embrace themes that are both personal and socially conscious. Solow's contributions to several recent documentaries, including Anti-Bias Curriculum *and* Healing the Wounds of Incest, *have allowed her to integrate her musical interests with her concern for child welfare. Her touring schedule often takes her through northern California and the Pacific Northwest.*

Jamie's a singer-songwriter and a dear friend of mine. Perhaps because we are so close, I feel that this guitar really captures a lot of her personality.

Its proportions are very feminine and strong, and I think the shape of the guitar works very gracefully from one end of it to the other— almost like one continuous note. But because it's got a bolt-on neck and the tuners are all on one side, you can also tell right away that it's definitely a musician's guitar. I feel that this was one of the most successful collaborations I've ever done in terms of the way it evokes its user, and Jamie bonded with the guitar almost immediately after I gave it to her.

1985 | 25½ inches   *Spruce* top *East Indian rosewood* body *mahogany* neck *ebony* fretboard

Chrissie
HYNDE

●

Lead singer, guitarist, and songwriter with her band the Pretenders, Hynde was raised in Ohio but moved to London in her early twenties to pursue a music career. After she united with three British musicians to form the Pretenders, the band released an eponymous debut album in 1980 that combined Hynde's deep, lyrical vocals with a richly textured, driving guitar sound. While continuing with the Pretenders, Hynde has also recorded with the reggae-inspired British group UB40.

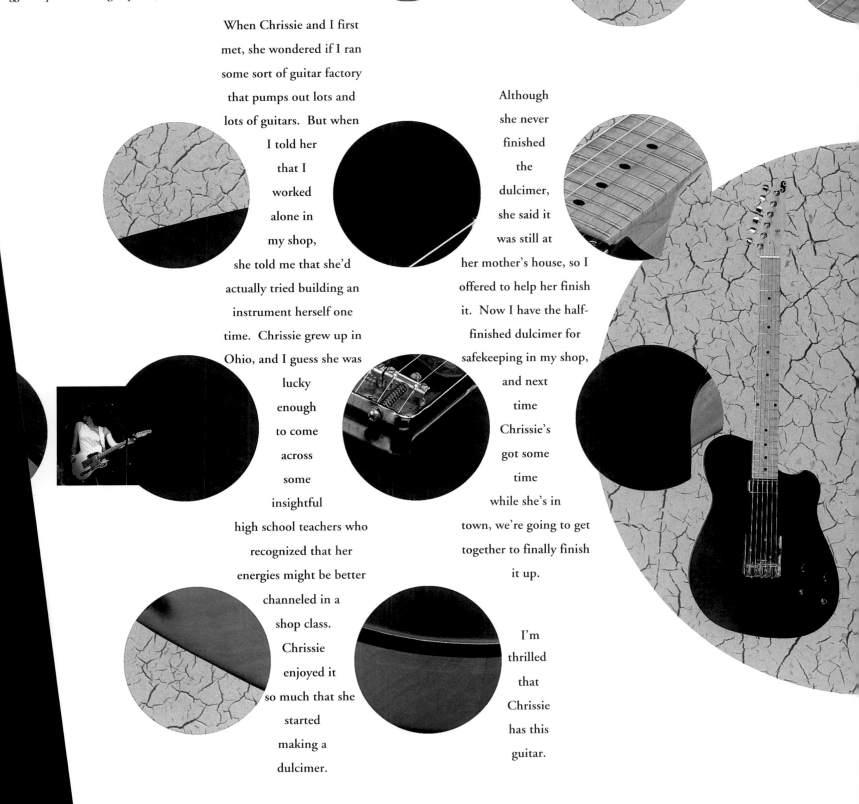

When Chrissie and I first met, she wondered if I ran some sort of guitar factory that pumps out lots and lots of guitars. But when I told her that I worked alone in my shop, she told me that she'd actually tried building an instrument herself one time. Chrissie grew up in Ohio, and I guess she was lucky enough to come across some insightful high school teachers who recognized that her energies might be better channeled in a shop class. Chrissie enjoyed it so much that she started making a dulcimer.

Although she never finished the dulcimer, she said it was still at her mother's house, so I offered to help her finish it. Now I have the half-finished dulcimer for safekeeping in my shop, and next time Chrissie's got some time while she's in town, we're going to get together to finally finish it up.

I'm thrilled that Chrissie has this guitar.

1990 | 25½ inches
Electric

Maple top, neck, and fretboard ***basswood*** body

ny
RDS

•

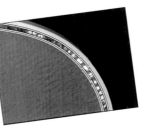

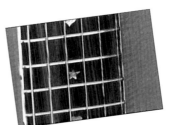

...s is a bass player, guitarist, singer, and producer who ...ding industry career as a member of Linda Ronstadt's ...band. Edwards has continued to perform with Ronstadt ...r career, while also contributing his distinctive Southern ...nd to albums by musicians such as Warren Zevon and ... He has produced three of Karla Bonoff's albums, and ... produced an album for Tom Kell.

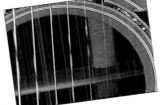

Kenny Edwards played a Ferrington baritone on "Blue Telephone" and "The Chapel," off Tom Kell's album *Angel Town* (Warner Brothers, 1992).

Kenny was an original member of Linda Ronstadt's Stone Poneys band, and he's been a real active session player and producer for a long time. He's one of the few people I know who actually grew up in Santa Monica, so his playing style embodies that classic Southern California sound from the troubadour days of the 1970s. This guitar was ordered as a wedding present for both Kenny and his wife, and it's built so that it can be strung up as either a left-handed or right-handed instrument depending upon the position of the saddle and the bolt-on neck. Kenny has always liked the style of a Martin 00028, so this guitar was sized and styled to look like that. It has a deep, traditional sound, but I think its presence and tone let you know that there's definitely a little bit of Ferrington kicking around in there as well.

Spruce top *Brazilian rosewood* body *mahogany* neck *ebony* fretboard

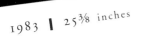

1983 | 25⅜ inches

Originally from Oklahoma, Cale has a highly fluid blues guitar style that, along with his gritty vocals has heavily influenced many other musicians, including Mark Knopfler of Dire Straits and Eric Clapton. Clapton's renditions of several Cale tunes, including "After Midnight" and "Cocaine," are archetypes of Cale's distinctive musical sound and have helped draw attention to his many talents.

I met J. J. Cale back in Nashville, and he's the guy who really set me on track building guitars that were different from everybody else's. I remember I once built this real nice copy of a Gibson mandolin, and when I showed it to John, he took one look at it and said, "It's good all right, but why make a copy? It's only gonna be as good as a Gibson, and there's an awful lot of them around already." That's when it really became clear to me that I ought to be trying to make guitars that nobody's ever seen before.

This guitar is one of my earliest. John bought it mainly to help give me a start as a luthier and to show his support for my abilities. He even gave me one of his old amplifiers just so I'd have something to use around my shop. The amp was worth more than the guitar he bought from me, but I think he looked upon it all as some sort of investment in my future.

John is amazingly clear-sighted and authentic, and I've found that his insights are invariably right on the money. It's real important for me to check in with him from time to time, because his opinions are like a mirror that always tells me if my work is moving along the right path.

1978 | 25⅜ inches   *Spruce* top *maple* body and neck *ebony* fretboard

Classical
GUITAR

This guitar is a prototype I built, to experiment with a split-top configuration. Normally a classical guitar is either a cedar top, which is bassy and warm-sounding, or a spruce top, which is loud and bright. When a classical musician wants to get a bright sound from a cedar-top guitar, the right hand picks with the fingernails. On a spruce-top guitar it's easy to get the bright sounds, but very difficult to get the warm, low sounds.

To make the treble notes brighter and the bass notes warmer on the classical guitar I used a harder wood—spruce—on the treble side and a softer wood—cedar—on the bass side.

By combining these two woods on the face of this guitar, I think that I've accomplished somewhat my goal of making a classical guitar that can be both bright *and* warm. This guitar also features several other unconventional ideas: a cutaway and a bolt-on neck.

David
LINDLEY

•

David Lindley is a multi-instrumentalist whose fiddle, steel, and guitar playing did a great deal to help shape the wailing, bittersweet sound of Jackson Browne's early music. As a session musician, he has performed with Rod Stewart, James Taylor, Ry Cooder, Linda Ronstadt, Iggy Pop, and Howard Jones. After traveling to Madagascar with Henry Kaiser to record the <u>World Out of Time</u> *album in 1991, Lindley began work on a current recording project with Hani Naser, a percussionist from Jordan.*

I've known David Lindley for a long time. He's played a lot of my guitars in the past, and he's such a good player that I wanted him to own something of mine.

David and I had talked for quite some time about my building this instrument—it's called a saz, a centuries-old Turkish instrument. The traditional ones that he owns, built in Turkey, have huge, bulbous backs carved from single pieces of wood. They're very difficult, if not impossible, to stand up and play, so he wanted me to create a modern, flat-back version.

I went out to David's house—he has a room full of these instruments—and we mixed and matched the qualities of each one to come up with this.

The frets are traditional and tied on and made of monofilament–fishing line. I put a little door in the back so he can get inside and arrange his acoustic-style pickup. I took some liberties with this, as I always do, and built it with a cutaway, so that it's like two sazes combined. The treble size is a small saz, and the bass size is a big saz. I particularly like the traditional-style tuners that I made; they look like mailboxes. David does lots of movie soundtrack work and these type of instruments, with long strings, make very atmospheric music because the notes ring for a long time.

1992 | 37¼ inches   *Spruce* and *ash* top *ash* body and fretboard *mahogany* neck
Saz

ROSSY

Paul Bert Rahasimanana is a multi-instrumentalist, singer, songwriter, and lead member of the Rossy group, the most popular and eclectic electric band on the island of Madagascar. The group started as youngsters, singing vakisoava (a very poetic, traditional call-and-response form that is popular in the slums of Tana) in the streets. In time they developed into an acoustic band and composed their own songs. They then added electric and nontraditional instruments, and today they travel all over Madagascar in their truck, playing electric "roots" music that combines musical elements of all six of the island's provinces. Rossy himself is known for his amazing vocals and mastery of several Malagasy string and wind instruments.

My friend Henry Kaiser brought Rossy and another musician from Madagascar to my shop to introduce me to them. They played for me a little–Rossy is probably one of the best musicians I've ever met.

Rossy told me about an instrument called a kabosy, and because his own wasn't very good, I offered to make him one, knowing that I could improve upon it. Rossy told me that he'd seen some kabosys that had a piece of wood glued onto the top, near the high strings, so that when you strum, the last thing you hit with the pick is that piece of wood, making a rhythm sound. I invented my own version of this by drilling a hole in the bridge that fits a rosewood dowel, sort of like a chopstick, that's suspended over the top with a moveable piece of wood wedged under it for tuning. Rossy loved my version, but unfortunately he took the piece out before shipping the kabosy for photography so it's not shown here.

Since they were playing a concert the next night and then leaving town, I started the kabosy around 7:00 p.m. that night and finished it in time for Rossy to play during the concert–I think it took about fourteen hours. Because of the poverty in Madagascar, the instruments there are very crude so this will be unique; the cutaway alone will revolutionize the playing. It was kind of nuts for me to build something that quick, but I couldn't miss out on building an instrument for a world-class musician. I feel like it's an honor.

Building instruments like the saz and kabosy keep me quick on my feet. When I built the kabosy, I didn't really even know what the name of it was. Every time I build a different instrument it seems I learn a little more about the guitar.

1990 | 25½ inches
Kabosy

Spruce top   *Brazilian rosewood* body and fretboard   *mahogany* neck

String
QUARTET

●

1992 | All instruments are a full 4/4 size   *Spruce* top *maple* body and neck ***ebony*** fretboard

The string quartet emerged from an idea I had about five years ago to build a jazz guitar with a top formed out of a thin piece of wood bent into an arch, rather than a solid arch curved out of a heavy piece of wood. I never built the jazz guitar, but when I thought about it, it seemed to me that the same process would work very well for bowed instruments.

I went to the UCLA music library and got a whole stack of books on Stradivari and the history of violin making, and learned that during Stradivari's lifetime, music wasn't written to be played above the point where the neck joins the body, or above the third or fourth position. Stradivari's design made sense for the music that was being played during his lifetime, but as composition progressed and people started to write music up in the high registers, a musician had to learn how to extend his hand over the top of the instrument to reach that end of the fretboard. At that point I think the traditional violin wasn't a practical design, because it constrained all but the most talented musicians who wanted to play those high notes.

I can't think of a single man-made object that hasn't changed its design in 300 years— except for the violin. The violin strings have changed, but the basic instrument is essentially identical to the thing that Stradivari was making three centuries ago. No two of Stradivari's violins were exactly the same, and I imagine that when he was in his workshop he was always trying to make each new one a little bit better than the last. The instruments have to evolve of their own accord, and I can't quite understand why people try to make new violins that sound exactly like ones that Stradivari might have built.

To provide access to the high registers of the fretboard, I sculpted my violins out on one side so that a musician can move his hand all the way up the neck while staying in the same playing position. The cutaway also makes it easier to play a vibrato in the high registers since the musician's fingers don't have to be straightened out to make the reach.

I also borrowed a few other ideas from the guitar world. I decided to use bolt-on necks like on an electric guitar to give even better access to the fretboard while also allowing the musician to adjust the tension on the neck. The tail pieces are adjustable so that you can easily change the tension, and the bodies use asymmetrical shapes that take care of a lot of the bad overtones you have in a typical violin, viola, or cello. The design is also very easy to construct, because the asymmetrical body eliminates the need to equalize the sound by carving out the top.

I started with a few prototype violins before moving on to the violas and the cello, and over time I began to refine my designs to the point where I felt I'd gotten a real lively sound out of the instruments. The tone of the cello is maybe a little bit too dark, but it's easy to go back and make it brighter by using a slightly thicker top and bracing. But creating a dark instrument is a hard thing to do, so I feel that I've already accomplished a difficult part by making it dark with a very deep presence.

The design of my string instruments is so different that the musicians who use them have told me that they easily captured a whole range of new positions that they'd never even imagined reaching before.

I could easily spend the rest of my life working on my string quartet, but my goal really is to make these instruments modern enough that some young kid dressed in high-top sneakers and blue jeans might look at a violin without feeling like he was going to be stuck in the trenches playing straight, classical music for the rest of his life. I love classical music, but you never know if there's some genius violin player out there right now who's spending his time banging away at an electric guitar. The instruments have to excite all kinds of people, and I thought that if I could make violins in modern shapes that actually work well as instruments, then maybe the next generation will actually consider playing the violin as much as kids now play the guitar.

I never really meant to be a guitar builder–as with a lot of people I know, my profession seemed to pick me. But now, when I look back and put the pieces together, it seems really obvious; everything points to this.

My mother sang all the time at home and my father has always loved music– he sang and played guitar at a young age. We have a photo, which I love, of my dad on his high school steps, guitar around his neck, with his two fellow bandmates. When I was barely walking, my dad worked for a local TV station and would some- times perform on one of its country music shows. My mother said that whenever my dad came on, I ran around the room in excitement and kissed the TV. Well before I was able to read, I could find any record I wanted just by the color of the label. I always loved music.

My father has had a lot of jobs, but he has always gravitated toward wood- working. From an early age I helped him in his cabinet shop back in Louisiana– we've worked together forever, it seems. My grandfather, Mack Ferrington, was very industrious–living in the country you have to make a lot of the things you need–and could fashion the most improbable things; they were crude, but they always seemed to work. There are times when I'm in a hurry to repair something and I catch myself just throwing it together, so it will work for the moment; I know it's my grandfather coming out–it's something in me I just can't deny. It's also that thing in my gut that has told me to go in a certain direction even though it's not an accepted way. I always use this improvisation in my work; it has helped me to be a different instrument builder.

I feel so lucky in this trade–I couldn't have invented a better niche for myself–and so fortunate to have my life attached to so wonderful a thing as the guitar. It's hard for me to put my feelings about the guitar into words; it's such a loved instrument. When I travel with one, people always smile and ask if I play, or what kind it is. After I tell them I'm a guitar builder, I always add, "It's a great way to be in the music business."

I also feel very fortunate to have known the musicians for whom I've built guitars, because the guitars wouldn't have been built without them. All of my best ideas have come from musicians, their music and talent enrich my life, and I thank them, all of them–the ones featured here as well as the ones not in the book.

There are so many people to thank that I feel like someone at the Oscars trying to squeeze everyone in—but I'll try.

I'd like to thank Randy Wood, from whom I learned my craft; he was always generous with his time and knowledge, and really put me on the right track. And also the late Doc Savage for introducing us.

Thanks to Malcolm Greer and Woody Kay for designing my logo.

The following friends whose support has been endless: Nauman Scott, J. D. Sloan, Paul Craft, Edward Foote, Lewis and Kathy Anderson, Ricky Skaggs, and Orville Schell.

Kenny Edwards for being my pal.

Jamie Solow for her loving soul.

Linda Ronstadt who's been such a dear friend for a long time now. Words fail me in thanking her; she knows anyway.

Every musician who's shown even a slight interest in me and my work, because that's what has kept me doing this—it sure wasn't for the money.

In regard to the book I would like to thank:

Nancy Skolos and Tom Wedell for their beautiful work and tireless energy.

Dear Kate Giel, my editor, who couldn't have worked harder or been a nicer friend through it all.

Everyone at Callaway Editions: Sandy Arrowsmith, Caissa Douwes, Martha Lazar, Toshi Masuda, Charlie Melcher, Monica Moran, Jin Park, José Rodriguez, True Sims, and Ivan Wong. Thank you, thank you, thank you.

Nicholas Callaway for his unwavering enthusiasm for what I do, for our project, and for putting out his hand and pulling me into another world.

Kind thanks to Ray DeMoulin and Joan Rosenberg at the Center for Creative Imaging.

Thanks to Federal Express for not damaging or losing any of the guitars.

I would like to dedicate this book to my family: my sister, Jan, and my brother, Dudley, and my parents, Amy and Loyd, whose love for me I've never doubted.

All of the CD compositions were originally performed for the book and composed by the musicians, unless otherwise noted. The individual tracks were mastered by George Massenberg and Ron Lewter at the Mastering Lab. The production and engineering of the tracks were by Danny Ferrington, unless otherwise noted.

Track 1
Richard Thompson
"The Job of Journey Work"
Traditional Celtic ballad
Producer: Mitchell Froom
Engineer: Tchad Blake
Richard Thompson performs
courtesy of Capitol Records, Inc.

Track 2
Rossy "Ovy Groovy"
Percussion: Rossy
Producer: Henry Kaiser
Engineer: Oliver DiCicco
Publisher: Ruminating
Music (ASCAP)

Track 3
Ry Cooder Melody
Engineer: Doug Diamond

Track 4
David Hidalgo "Li'l King
of Everything"
written by David Hidalgo
and Louie Perez
Producer: Mitchell Froom
Engineer: Tchad Blake
Publisher: Davince Music/
No K O Music (BMI)
Administered by Bug Music
David Hidalgo performs
courtesy of Slash/Warner
Brothers, Inc.

Track 5
Reeves Gabrels
"J'aime M'asseoir
dans Mon Territoire"
Producer: Reeves Gabrels
Engineer: Tom Dubé
Publisher: Reeves
Gabrels Music

Track 6
Stephen Bishop
"Rebecca"
Publisher: Stephen Bishop
Music Publishing Co.
Administered by Careers–
BMG Music Publishing, Inc. (BMI)

Track 7
J. J. Cale "Danny's Song"
Publisher: Danny Ferrington Music

Track 8
Michael Ward "Dolores"
Producer: Michael Ward
and Dennis Herring
Engineer: Dennis Herring
Publisher: Dan Is Here/New
Envoy Music (ASCAP)
Michael Ward performs
courtesy of Capitol
Records, Inc.

Track 9
Randy Jacobs
"Miss Faye"
Sax: David McMurry
Producer: Don Was
Engineer: Rik Pekkonen
Publisher: Ran Dog (ASCAP)

Track 10
Phoebe Snow
"Old Country Rock"
written by Stefan Grossman
and Aurora Block
Producer: Phoebe Snow
Engineer: Wayne Yurgelun
Publisher: Heathside
Music, Ltd. (PRS)
Adm. in the U.S.A.
and Canada by
Careers-BMG Music
Publishing, Inc. (BMI)
All rights reserved
Used by permission

Track 11
Neil Finn Melody
Produced and engineered by
Neil Finn
Neil Finn performs courtesy of
Capitol Records, Inc.

Track 12
David Lindley
"Elvis Is Alive"
Publisher: Neuoleum Music

Track 13
Kenny Edwards
"Afternoon at George's"

Track 14
Michael Landau "Judy"
Produced and engineered by
Michael Landau

Track 15
Albert Lee Instrumental

Track 16
J. D. Souther Melody
Publisher: Dog Ranch Music

Track 17
Henry Kaiser "It Happened
One Night"
Produced and engineered by
Henry Kaiser

Track 18
Elvis Costello playing the
Ferrington guitar trio
"May 17th"
Produced and engineered by
Elvis Costello
Elvis Costello performs
courtesy of Warner
Brothers, Inc.

Track 19
String quartet
"Violins du Jour"
Performers: Joel Derouin
on first violin; David
Campbell on second violin;
Larry Corbett on cello;
Novi Novog on viola
Producer and string
arranger: David Campbell
Engineer: Rik Pekkonen
Publisher: DRC Music
(ASCAP)

Track 20
Don Was "Home Sweet
Home"/"Baby Love"/"A
Tribute to Nineteenth
Century America and
the Supremes"
"Home Sweet Home"
written by Henry R. Bishop
and John W. Payne
"Baby Love" written by
Eddie Holland, Brian
Holland, and Lamont Dozier
Produced and engineered
by Don Was
"Baby Love" Publisher:
Stone Agate Music © 1964

Ferrington Guitars was produced by Callaway Editions.
Nicholas Callaway was the Editorial Director.
Kate Giel was the Editor, with assistance from Martha Lazar.
True Sims was the Production Director,
with assistance from Ivan Wong.

Todd Lappin compiled the plate commentary and the short biographies of the musicians.

Barbara Bergeron was the free-lance copy editor.

Wendy Wolf was the Editor at HarperCollins, with assistance from Eileen Campion.

The design and photography were by Nancy Skolos and Thomas Wedell of Skolos/Wedell, Inc., Boston,
with production assistance from Jennifer Ernst. The book's pages were designed on the PREMIER™
Image Enhancement System at Kodak's Center for Creative Imaging in Camden, Maine,
with technical assistance from Bob Cole and Peter Koons.

More than fifty guitars were photographed, and over 1,000 sheets of 4 x 5
Ektachrome 100 Plus film were exposed. In addition, 4 x 5s were produced of
various materials such as wood, cloth, metal, and lighting effects to be used as
backgrounds in the compositions.

To assemble the spread compositions on the Premier, the individual 4 x 5s
of guitars and background materials were scanned by a Premier film reader
at 2,000 pixels per inch.

Before the guitar images were
pasted into the composition,
each image had to be masked, or
silhouetted, on the system.

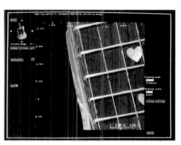
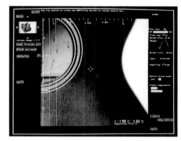

The masks were drawn at a
zoomed-in scale to ensure perfect
edges; approximately fifty full-
screen areas were required to mask
the perimeter of one guitar.

After the images were
masked, they were
retouched to remove dust
and blemishes.

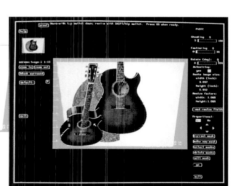

Compositions were assembled background to foreground; each cut and sub-assembly
was post-processed in the computer.

Each composition contained approximately six images; the data file for one image
comprised approximately 247 megabytes. The Premier system utilized up to 4.3
gigabytes of disk storage to assemble one spread.

Spread compositions were archived onto 8mm videotape, and output onto
8 x 10-inch Ektachrome using the Premier film writer, which has a resolution of 1,000 pixels per inch.

Separations were made by Laserscan, Inc. of Phoenix, Arizona. The 8 x 10-inch Ektachromes were scanned using a DS608 Scanner.
To match the original art, color corrections and retouching were performed by Nick Yannuzzi, Systems Manager, on Laserscan's Scitex
C.E.P.S. using both the Righttouch Workstation and Imager II. The 200-line-screen separation film was output on the
Raystart Image Plotter.

The text was composed using Aldus PageMaker®. The typeface for the text and display is Adobe Garamond™; the numbers and folios are
from the Adobe Garamond Expert Collection™. The type was output by High Resolution, Inc., Camden, Maine.

The book was printed in Portland, Oregon by Graphic Arts Center and bound in Nashville, Tennessee by Nicholstone.

The plates were printed in four-color offset lithography on 100 lb. Vintage Glossy text. The book was smyth-sewn in
sixteen-page signatures. The jacket was printed in four colors with a liquid UV lamination.

The compact disc was manufactured by WEA Manufacturing, Inc., Olyphant, Pennsylvania. Its holder was made by
Williams Industries, Inc., Shelbyville, Indiana.

The printing and binding of the book were supervised by True Sims and Toshiya Masuda.

First Edition

Library of Congress Cataloging-in-Publication Data

Ferrington, Danny
Ferrington Guitars: featuring the custom-made guitars of master luthier
Danny Ferrington. Art direction, design, and photography, Nancy Skolos and
Thomas Wedell. Introduction, Linda Ronstadt. Profile, Orville Schell.
Editor, Kate Giel. Editorial Director, Nicholas Callaway.–1st ed.
    p.   cm.
ISBN 0-06-016897-8 (hardcover)–ISBN 0-06-099268-9 (CD)
    1. Guitar makers–United States. 2. Guitar–Pictorial works. 3. Ferrington, Danny.
    I. Ferrington, Danny. II. Wedell, Thomas. III. Skolos, Nancy. IV. Schell, Orville.
    V. Giel, Kate. VI. Callaway, Nicholas. VII. Title.
    ML 1015. G9558   1992
    787. 87 1973–dc20   92-52605

    92 93 94 95 96   10 9 8 7 6 5 4 3 2 1

The photographs of the musicians appearing in the plate section were provided
by the following:

Photographs of Mike Campbell, Neil Finn, Reeves Gabrels, David Hidalgo,
Jamie Solow, and Richard Thompson © 1992 Thomas Wedell.

Photographs of Kurt Cobain, Kenny Edwards, Randy Jacobs, Michael Landau, Albert Lee,
Michael Ward, and Don Was by Danny Ferrington © 1992 Callaway Editions.

Photographs from Outline Press, New York: Ry Cooder © 1988 John Livzey;
Elvis Costello © 1991 Frank W. Ockenfels; David Lindley © 1988 Gary Moss;
John Prine © 1992 Brian Smith; J. D. Souther © 1990 Neal Preston.

Photographs of Hoyt Axton provided by Mae Boren Axton; J. J. Cale provided by
Rosebud Management; Rosanne Cash © Ron Keith; Rodney Crowell © David Roth;
Little Jimmy Dickens provided by Tater-Patch Productions; Roddy Frame provided by
Andrew Catlin Publicity; Crystal Gayle © Empire Studio; Emmylou Harris ©
Caroline Greyshock; Henry Kaiser by Banning Eyre; Linda Ronstadt © Robert Blakeman;
Rossy by Banning Eyre; Phoebe Snow by Martha Lazar © 1992 Callaway Editions.

Photographs from London Features International, New York and London:
Michael Anthony © Rick Mikels; Stephen Bishop © Ron Wolfson; Jackson Browne ©
Kevin Mazur; Carlene Carter © Ron Wolfson; Chris Difford © Robin Kaplan;
Chrissie Hynde © Ilpo Musto; Nick Lowe © Gie Knaeps.